GENERAL GRIVAS
ON
GUERRILLA WARFARE

GEORGE GRIVAS

GENERAL GRIVAS
ON
GUERRILLA WARFARE

Translated by A. A. Pallis

FREDERICK A. PRAEGER, *Publishers*

NEW YORK · WASHINGTON

BOOKS THAT MATTER

Published in the United States of America in 1965
by Frederick A. Praeger, Inc., Publishers
111 Fourth Avenue, New York 3, N.Y.

All rights reserved

First published in Athens under the title
  Agon EOKA kai Antartopolemos

© 1962 George Grivas-Dighenis

English translation copyright © 1964 by Longmans, Green and Co., Ltd.

Library of Congress Catalog Card Number: 65-14587

Printed in the United States of America

This book is dedicated to the
Greek Officer
GEORGE GRIVAS-DIGHENIS

Contents

APPENDIX

Foreword

The present study is based on my personal military experience to date. It does not attempt to examine every form of guerrilla warfare nor all questions relating to it. Some of these I have not touched upon because one can find and study them in relevant military manuals or elsewhere.

In these few pages I have endeavoured to set forth, mainly for the benefit of the soldier, firstly, the way in which I solved the various problems which confronted me during the Cyprus liberation campaign which I directed for four and a half years and, secondly, the strategic and tactical conclusions to which I was led on guerrilla warfare in general. Anyone who studies the present work and compares it with accounts of similar struggles will, no doubt, find striking differences. As I point out, each struggle outside the type of conventional warfare has its own special characteristics and consequently its peculiar strategy and tactics.[1]

My main aim is to draw attention to guerrilla warfare as a form of combat which might be employed in some future conflict, as well as to the methods which it uses. For the various situations of which Asia is today the theatre and which may tomorrow be repeated elsewhere, under various conditions of unorthodox warfare, should warn us of what can happen even now if things go on as at present, but also of what the future may hold in store for us.

The present shows us that the Communist bloc, under the cloak of undeclared war and using forms of combat that do not come under the rules of conventional warfare, is continually gaining strategical ground, infiltrating wherever it can, slowly but surely and relentlessly. The future should make us reflect on the probable shape of a new world war. For the continuous and vigorously pursued discovery of new, terribly destructive weapons is bound to influence the deployment of military resources on the strategic and tactical plane – a deployment which, in my opinion, will take the form of dispersion and concealment in depth and underground.

[1] To help the reader complete his knowledge of guerrilla warfare I refer him to the following works: *Mao Tse-tung on Guerrilla Warfare*, translated and with an introduction by Samuel B. Griffith (Praeger, 1961); *Che Guevara on Guerrilla Warfare*, with an introduction by Harries-Clichy Peterson (Praeger, 1961); and George K. Tanham, *Communist Revolutionary Warfare: The Vietminh in Indochina* (Praeger, 1961).

The military experts, if they wish to avoid being taken by surprise, should study the present so as to be able to forecast the future. For a leader's greatest attribute is to prepare the ground and take his opponent by surprise while himself avoiding falling into a trap.

We should realize that unorthodox kinds of warfare are bound to be employed on a very wide scale in any future war. It is therefore essential that these be studied and taught in our military academies – perhaps there should even be established a special school of guerrilla warfare – and the matter should receive the special attention of the Staffs in every country.

We all know that the general shape of future hostilities within a country is the concern of every government in consultation with its military advisers.

But modern technical progress and developments in the international field render it essential for the political leaders, whose basic aim must be national security, to give more thought to strategic policy, which logically cannot and should not be left to fall entirely on the shoulders of the Services. I do not wish to enlarge on this theme in the present survey, for I would have much to say on the matter in the context of NATO.

GENERAL GRIVAS
ON
GUERRILLA WARFARE

1. Guerrilla Warfare as an Instrument of Policy

'War is merely a rather drastic method of giving
expression to policy, of which it is a continuation.'

CLAUSEWITZ

Guerrilla warfare is a form of war and, as such, a suitable weapon in the hands of nations and states for the promotion of their national military policy whether offensive or defensive.

There is nothing new in this form of warfare. It has been, from time immemorial, the means which weak, subject peoples have used against their masters to recover their freedom.

The Balkan peoples threw off the yoke of the then all-powerful Ottoman Empire in risings which took the form of guerrilla wars. The Greek War of Independence of 1821 began as a guerrilla war. Although subsequently its forces grew greatly in strength, the bands of irregulars became organized on military lines and, with the help of foreign Philhellenes who came to Greece, a small number of regular corps were formed, nevertheless the methods generally employed by that revolutionary army were guerrilla methods. For, faced by a vastly more powerful army, the weaker side cannot employ the conventional methods of warfare, but is bound to adopt new ones which will make up for its inferiority in numbers and material means.

During the Second World War resistance movements spontaneously broke out in the countries occupied by the Axis and they employed the methods of guerrilla warfare.

After the war Russia in particular resorted to this form of warfare as an instrument of foreign policy, seeking, by skilful infiltration, to win an ideological victory, especially in countries where, through the miserable condition of the masses, and the presence of colonial or dictatorial régimes, the desire for freedom as well as the readiness to fight for liberation were acutely developed. Mao Tse Tung's China, Cuba, Laos, North Vietnam, Kenya, etc., are characteristic examples.

Latin America today is like an overheated boiler, with the Soviet Union's finger on the safety-valve. Perhaps the only post-war uprisings which were not inspired by Communist ideology but were solely prompted by the desire for national independence were the Algerian and Cypriot revolts.

The Cypriot liberation movement, in particular, refused to accept co-operation with Communism, nor would it allow the latter to exploit it. For this reason it was fiercely opposed by the local Communists who therefore co-operated with the British authorities. Communists will never forgive a movement which, unaided, raises the standard of resistance to the oppressor; for they want to have the monopoly of any struggle of this kind, in view of the fact that their ulterior and sole aim is to make party capital out of every national movement. Their dogma, as pronounced by Stalin, is: 'The Communist parties are the only ones left who are ready to raise the national flag and go forward with it.'

Communist infiltration and victory through revolutionary action in the form of guerrilla warfare are today regarded by the Soviet Union as being the most effective methods for the following reasons:

1. They promote the more general Soviet strategy by securing strategic areas which will serve later in case of need as offensive or defensive bases, in the event of a local or general conflict.

2. The Soviet Union is no longer invulnerable as she was in the past, owing to her vast territory, her climatic conditions and her position in relation to her probable adversaries. Consequently, instead of risking a total war which, with the present nuclear weapons, would possibly entail her own destruction, she seeks to extend her influence through restricted local wars which she instigates, though she leaves it to others to fight them, so that even in the event of failure the results may be relatively harmless to herself.

3. The Soviet Union uses a very effective weapon, which counts for a great deal in the struggle: the people's deep-seated feeling of social injustice and love of freedom.

4. The Soviet Union is in a position to act even in distant countries not adjacent to her territory, and to keep the struggle going there for a long time, without there being any need for her to resort to direct intervention, which might expose her in the international field and cause her to incur responsibilities as a disturber of world peace, with all the consequences that might arise therefrom.

5. There exist in nearly all countries Communist parties whose followers are able to work, prepare and eventually actively assist liberation or resistance movements.

6. The Western powers today are incapable of dealing with this kind of warfare, either because they have not got the appropriate organization, or for psychological reasons, or on grounds of expediency,

whereas they are in all circumstances prepared to face a conventional war, as has happened on more than one occasion. One may ask oneself what would have been the outcome in Korea had Mao's Chinese, instead of committing open aggression, resorted to guerrilla warfare, and whether, in such a case, America and her allies would have intervened on the side of South Korea.

The Chinese realized their mistake, for since then they have never risked a war of the conventional type but have pursued their aggression in the form of guerrilla warfare in South East Asia, South Vietnam and Laos.

Finally, we should take into account two other advantages of this kind of struggle: firstly, the saving in manpower and material as well as money, as compared with a conventional war (it only requires very limited means to enable one to stand up to a very powerful opponent, as was the case in Cyprus); secondly, the limited vulnerability to nuclear weapons, seeing that a guerrilla war does not involve targets of nuclear importance. It goes without saying that in any future war the use of nuclear weapons must inevitably impose a dispersal of one's resources. Guerrilla warfare, because of its very nature and methods of combat, automatically leads to such dispersal.

2. What are the Prospects for Guerrilla Warfare?

Guerrilla warfare may occur in the following two forms:

1. As an independent military action within a country, which has been prepared in or outside that country and has either been provoked by social causes or comes as the result of a movement for national liberation.

2. As part of a country's or a coalition's general strategic plan and related to a conventional war arising out of a local or general conflict.

It is therefore obvious that future strategy will be affected by this kind of military operation, and all strategic planning will have to foresee and prepare for not only guerrilla tactics inside the enemy's territory but also the means of counteracting similar action on the part of the opponent on friendly territory.

Both of the above cases call for separate examination in order to draw the necessary conclusions in regard to the strategy and tactics to be adopted.

It is not an easy task. For whereas in the case of conventional war there exist certain general principles and operational methods, whether strategic or tactical, which may be found in the text-books, in the case of a guerrilla war there is no special type, only the special circumstances under which it may occur, and each one of these special circumstances calls for its own special strategy and tactics. Thus, for instance, the resistance movements in Greece and Yugoslavia during the Second World War present no kind of analogy to the liberation movement in Cyprus, just as the latter bears no resemblance to the insurrectionary movement in Algeria, though both were actuated by the same motive, namely, the throwing off of colonial rule.

The liberation struggle of the Algerian people has nothing in common with Mao's Chinese social revolution or with the revolution in Cuba. Consequently, the views and facts set forth in these pages are not intended as ready-made prescriptions but are merely intended to give a general idea of guerrilla warfare and to draw attention to certain questions of a strategic and tactical nature.

It is for the statesmen and military advisers in each country to determine the strategy and tactics to be applied in every case. When I drew up the General Plan of action for the Cyprus liberation campaign I had no model before me nor did I seek to follow blindly what had happened in Greece or elsewhere under similar circumstances of revolutionary action. I applied certain general principles and methods which were applicable to the special case of Cyprus. In my opinion, that was one of the principal reasons for our military success.

PART II

3. The Cyprus Liberation Campaign

STRATEGIC CONCEPTION OF THE CAMPAIGN

THE STRATEGIC OBJECTIVE

In my General Plan[1] of insurrectionary action in Cyprus I defined this objective as follows:

'By deeds of heroism and self-sacrifice to draw the attention of international public opinion, especially among the allies of Greece. . . .

'By continuously harassing the British in Cyprus, we must show that we are firmly determined not to yield, whatever the sacrifice, but that on the contrary we are prepared to continue until international diplomacy exercised through the United Nations, and the British in particular, are compelled to examine the Cyprus problem and reach a speedy settlement in accordance with the aspirations of the Cypriot people and the whole Greek nation.'

I also wrote in my General Plan:

'It should not be supposed that by these means we should expect to impose a total defeat on the British forces in Cyprus. Our purpose is to win a moral victory through a process of attrition, by harassing, confusing and finally exasperating the enemy forces, with the object of achieving our main aim as defined [above] . . .'

This clear strategic objective remained unchanged right to the end of the struggle and guided all our actions.

ORIGINAL STRATEGIC PLAN

I studied and took into consideration the following factors:

Terrain. Cyprus is an island with an area of 3,584 square miles, which can easily be blockaded by the opponent by sea and air and consequently can be cut off from all external supplies. The nature of the terrain did not facilitate the conduct of any conventional guerrilla operations. The two mountain massifs – Olympus and Pentadactylos – are everywhere easily negotiable on foot and are crossed in all directions by tarred roads. Troops can be transported by motor vehicle from the capital, Nicosia, to any point in the island in the space of

---

[1] This plan, which was drawn up in Greece before my departure for Cyprus, is to be found in the Appendix, pp. 91-95.

about two hours. Finally, the small area made it possible for the British to conduct frequent and detailed searches.

Population. The inhabitants had no experience of war because the Cypriots had no military service. Though by nature peace-loving, the Greeks of Cyprus, who form 80 per cent of the population, lived in the belief and the steadfast hope that some day someone would be found to raise the standard of insurrection and win them their freedom. This live and unshakeable yearning for freedom which inspired all Cypriots was my principal trump card.

Arms. These were non-existent and had to be imported, at any rate the bulk of them, before the beginning of the struggle, because later it would be very difficult to bring any in. The capture of arms from the enemy in sufficient quantities did not appear to be a practicable proposition.

The Opponent. The enemy had unlimited resources at his disposal and complete control of the island.

The strategic objective, as defined, and the other factors mentioned above formed the basis and dictated the lines of my 'General Plan' which consisted of the following:

1. *Combat operations.* Sabotage of government installations and posts.

Surprise attacks by a small number of highly mobile combat units against the British forces.

Each of these missions would have to be entrusted to special units which, at any rate at the outset, would have to be small in numbers, both because of lack of equipment and trained personnel, and for precautionary reasons, to enable me easily to modify my plan in accordance with developments with the greatest possible speed.

At first I concentrated my main effort on sabotage. As I wrote in my General Plan: 'Because of the difficulty of conducting a systematic, large-scale armed guerrilla campaign and in view of the fact that the territory is not capable of absorbing large guerrilla forces, the main weight of the campaign will be placed on sabotage.' Further on I say: 'I do not believe that the number of shock groups should be more than [the figure laid down in the Plan], at any rate initially. For a higher number would make it harder for them to hide or to get away in the event of attack. The terrain should appear empty so as to make discovery difficult by British search forces; passing through the enemy lines and escape will also thus be facilitated.'

However I did not exclude the possibility, should suitable con-

6

ditions present themselves, of the guerrilla armed struggle developing on a bigger and more intensive scale than originally planned.

'Should events take a more favourable turn,' I wrote in the General Plan, 'and always provided that sufficient weapons are available, one should not exclude the possibility of the armed struggle increasing both in scale and intensity.

'Action under the [two] forms mentioned above [sabotage and armed attack], if it is to attain its object, cannot be confined to minor and intermittent operations against insignificant targets but must involve a vigorous and continuous campaign, aimed at getting important results.'

2. *The laying down, in general terms, of subsidiary plans for passive resistance, information, supplies etc.*

ORGANIZATION OF THE CAMPAIGN[1]

PREPARATION

Taking into consideration the special conditions of the struggle, as outlined above, the preparatory stage passed through two phases.

The first consisted of two personal reconnaissances which I made in Cyprus. On the basis of these, the General Plan was drawn up, the methods to be employed during the struggle were studied, the first combat units were formed and arrangements made for taking delivery of the arms to be sent from Greece. On my return to Greece I devoted my whole efforts to getting these supplies together. This phase lasted from June 1951 to November 1954.

The second phase began with my arrival in Cyprus, which took place in the greatest secrecy. It was devoted to organizing and training the first combat units, to the selection and reconnaissance of the first targets and to the drawing up of the plans of attack against these targets. This phase covered the period between November 1954 and 1 April 1955, which date marked the beginning of the struggle. Field-Marshal Harding, in articles published in the *Daily Telegraph*, admits that at the time when we started operations, almost nothing was known to the British authorities in Cyprus about our organization and the names of its leaders.

The main feature which characterized both phases was secrecy.

---

[1] Details concerning the application of the methods referred to in the present chapter will be found in *The Chronicle of the Cypriot Struggle*, soon to be published in Greece.

Thanks to this, we were able to take the enemy completely by surprise, so much so that, by the admission of the British authorities in the island, several months after we went into action they still possessed no positive information about the Organization. On 20 June 1955 the British Commander of the Cyprus Police admitted to journalists that he was completely in the dark about the Organization – E O K A – and was not on its tracks.

Had the British got wind of what we were doing during the preparatory stage, it would have been impossible to transport the arms to the island, and the struggle, even if it broke out at all, would have been nipped in the bud. It is a generally recognized truth that careful preparation and securing the element of surprise are half the secret of success. The other half depends on skilful leadership. In my opinion, given these two factors, numbers are not of such great importance in guerrilla warfare. It is also significant that our opponent, strategically, was taken by surprise: a fact due not only to the secrecy of our preparations and of our first operations, but also to his lack of preparedness and the unco-ordinated nature of his actions, both tactically and from the point of view of organization, that might have enabled him to cope with such a struggle. Consequently, the enemy wasted a good deal of time in preparations to enable him to take action, with the known unfortunate results. The British army in Cyprus, owing to the nature of its organization and formation, was a clumsy weapon completely lacking in the training necessary for this kind of fighting. The same applied to the police who, in addition, were not equipped with suitable arms, which were only hastily sent out from England and distributed to them several months after we had gone into operation. The British, in order to train their forces for guerrilla warfare, carried out their first joint army and police exercises in the Kyrenia area at the beginning of June 1955. According to information supplied to us by a member of the police force who took part, the tactics employed were the following: fast-moving transport was sent out along the roads to cut off the retreat of the supposed guerrilla groups, while other sections advanced over the mountain-tops in order gradually to throw a tight cordon round the supposed area of flight of the guerrillas. Troops surrounded every village, because the inhabited areas were regarded as providing the main hiding-places where the guerrillas could conceal themselves and receive food from the villagers. Helicopters flew above the area of operations to notify the troops of any guerrilla movements.

8

The results of these exercises, as reported to me, were far from encouraging for the British, who found that:

1. It was impossible to cut off all communication by road.
2. It was extremely difficult to search mountain terrain, especially when thickly covered with forest.
3. It was also difficult to carry out effective search of the villages, given the hostility of the inhabitants towards the British forces.

ORGANIZATION OF FORCES AND RESOURCES

My main task was to create the instrument or instruments needed to facilitate the execution of my plan, and to make the best use of them. My efforts began during the preparatory stage and continued, at an accelerated pace, throughout the duration of the struggle. I state below what were the main organizational themes I had to face, and how I dealt with each one.

ORGANIZATION OF COMBAT UNITS: The struggle in Cyprus was of a quite special nature. Secrecy and the need to secure the element of surprise made it necessary to avoid starting large-scale organization too early.

The organization had to be carried out in Cyprus itself, on British-occupied territory where we could not form a base of our own. The organization of a revolutionary army in Greece itself to invade Cyprus was not possible for the following reasons: the Greek Government would not allow the organization of any such force on Greek territory in order to avoid an open breach with Great Britain; an invasion of Cyprus would have to be either by a forced landing, for which we did not have the necessary means, or by the secret disembarkation of small sections, with only the slightest chances of success, if at all. Further, it would be extremely difficult for any such preparation to escape the attention of the British agents in Greece. For this reason I ruled out the organization even of small bodies and their dispatch, by sections, to Cyprus.

Consequently, we sacrificed numbers for the sake of surprise. There could be no question of disposing of a large or even adequate strength, because of our great inferiority in resources. My advantage would lie in the use of suitable tactics which would enable me, on each occasion and within the necessary time-limit, to have the upper hand.

It followed that the combat units would be organized by degrees. Initially we organized some sabotage groups in the towns. These did

9

not exceed twenty in number. Later on, in July-August 1955, I brought into action a few groups of guerrillas. As my resources increased, I proceeded to strengthen both sabotage and guerrilla units. But our resources were extremely limited. Arms were imported from Greece under great difficulties, in driblets, either through the parcel post or through our couriers. Consequently, I was later forced to use shotguns, a quantity of which I seized from their owners in a single night. I used them to form special detachments, called 'Shotgun Commando Groups' (known, under their Greek initials, as O K T[1]). They gave excellent results in ambushes.

As regards munitions, at the start we were very short but gradually we succeeded in supplying our own needs. Certain quantities we were able to salvage from ships which had been sunk off the coasts of Cyprus during the Second World War. Others we manufactured using explosives obtainable in Cyprus itself and sold in the shops. We even produced such things as land mines (see Appendix pp. 101-6 for the various mixtures used as well as the types of bomb and mine we manufactured).

In this way we gradually succeeded, under fantastically difficult conditions, in forming our invisible army which covered the whole island. This army was everywhere, in the smallest village, in the furthest point of the island. It was present everywhere but never showed itself. As for its numbers, it is difficult even for me to say. For, ultimately, because of our system, every Greek Cypriot, from the smallest child to old men and women, belonged to our army, and fulfilled a mission either as a combatant or in the auxiliary services. Furthermore, the secrecy maintained throughout the Organization was so perfect that although our opponent managed to learn about its general lines, he never succeeded in discovering the essential features of the whole secret machinery and consequently was unable to break it up and crush it.

At first, the enemy tried to dislocate the Organization by arresting dynamic elements, mostly young people, but without success. Later, he resorted to mass arrests (2,100 Greeks were rounded up in one night), but again with no result. Our secret lay above all in the choice of our fighters, in our system of organization and in the tactics followed, which made it difficult for the enemy to capture them. Further, any

---

[1] *Translator's Note.* Wherever the abbreviated titles of formations occur in the text, the Greek initials are given.

gaps in the ranks, from whatever cause, were at once filled from our reserves which we were careful always to have ready up to strength.

PARTICIPATION OF THE POPULATION: A revolutionary movement and a guerrilla war, in particular, stand no chance of success, whatever the qualities of their leader, unless they have the complete and unreserved support of the majority of the country's inhabitants, for it is to them that the movement will turn for assistance of every kind (cadres and fighters, hiding places, concealment of equipment and men, liaison agents, food supplies, propaganda, etc.). My own military career has taught me that the collapse of the front usually begins from the rear. Consequently, I devoted my attention to organizing the population in order not only to get it actively to participate in the struggle but also to enable it to hold out, seeing that our struggle was above all a matter of time and endurance.

Already on 23 March 1955, in a letter addressed to Archbishop Makarios in which I set out my General Plan of organization, I foretold the total participation of the people in the armed struggle through uprisings and disturbances. I concluded as follows:

'Should the plan I have sketched above, namely, of acts of sabotage, attacks on police stations, activity of guerrilla bands, etc., be crowned with success, then I shall organize a general uprising of the youth in the towns and in the rural districts, in the form of aggressive demonstrations in which the organized population will take part.'

For four years, alongside the armed campaign, there went on a continuous struggle as to which of the two opponents would win the population over to his side. The weapon used by the British was force. But it was found that the harsher the measures resorted to by the British, the more the population became estranged from them and inclined to our side. Civilized peoples cannot be won over through violence, only through good treatment and a just and paternal administration. The representatives of Britain in Cyprus, both soldiers and civilians, behaved towards the inhabitants with an animosity which was far from politic. They were completely deficient in that understanding of the mass psychology which is so essential a factor of success in such circumstances. They showed by their behaviour that they had been unable to penetrate the motives which had impelled the Cypriot people to rise up against them. This was a serious disadvantage. All the British Governors in Cyprus failed miserably in this respect. In my *Memoirs* I have written an objective criticism of the two Governors, Harding and Foot, and of their behaviour towards the population. We, on the other hand, used methods which were in the main based on mass psychology, we employed persuasion, we set an example of endurance in the face of danger and privation, but above all we stimulated the people's faith in the justice of their cause. Throughout the struggle I never ceased for a single moment to strive to hold the people's moral support. In this I was completely successful and my appeal always met with full response on the part of all the Greeks of the island, whatever the sacrifice demanded. Every call on my part was regarded by the population as an order to fulfil a national duty. My proclamations were looked upon as sacred documents. Every man hastened to acquaint himself with their contents and to comply with them. My orders overrode the laws of the local British administration. In this way, I won the confidence of the Greek population of the island and every Greek Cypriot became a member of E O K A. The reply which the Mayor of Nicosia, Mr Dervis, gave the British Governor is a good example. When the latter demanded that the inhabitants help to arrest members of E O K A, the Mayor replied: 'But we all belong to E O K A.'

The success of any revolutionary movement depends, amongst other things, on political vision, skill and diplomatic tact towards the population. Who wins over the people, has won half the battle. It is, of course, one of the qualities of a leader to distinguish what means he must employ for that end. One can lay down no rules, no ready-made prescriptions.

I wish to stress that in the choice of my first key men I never made any distinction of social class, either among townsmen or villagers, and this continued to be my policy throughout. Communist revolutions usually start from the masses who have economic grievances, that is, among the workmen and peasants; the movement makes them all kinds of promises, and with the support of these classes imposes itself on the rest. But national liberation movements must express the will of the whole people. Liberation struggles succeed only when they find a response among the people. True to these ideas, I started my struggle by choosing my key men from the towns where I found the youth better organized, with a more marked patriotic enthusiasm for the fight, which was in time communicated to the whole of the island.

I cannot say which class contributed most. For the whole Greek population of the island rallied round the Organization as a single man, burning with desire for combat, and every man gave what he could. The one exception was, needless to say, the Communist leadership, the mass of whose followers, however, deserted them: the only ones who adhered by them were a few party officials and a small number of fanatics, whereas the great majority condemned their leaders and joined in E O K A's struggle.

The organization of the population, as described later (see pp. 28-30), was so markedly successful that the whole Greek population of Cyprus, roused from its slumbers, obeyed the order and took part in the fight, regardless of sex and age. In the villages the women formed resistance groups and stood up to the British attacks, some of them falling victims to enemy bullets. In the towns young girls formed sabotage and assault groups. Some of them were arrested and imprisoned, while many women carried out dangerous missions as liaisons or for the transport of arms.[1]

At Geneva, where I was asked to speak on the Cyprus liberation campaign, I was asked by someone the following question: 'What you have told us about organizing the population is all very well, but don't forget you had to deal with the British. But what would happen if we had to do with Russians who, apart from the much more rigorous measures they would be likely to take in order to overawe the population, might even go so far as to deport all the inhabitants of an insurrectionary region?'

My reply: 'A people, who are determined to rise against their masters and have the faith to continue the struggle, must always reckon with the harsh measures which will be taken against them, and

[1] It is difficult for me to mention all the acts of heroism, individual or collective, of the population, because they are so many. I single out one or two clashes between unarmed peasants and the British armed forces, which are to the credit of the Greek Cypriot population:

1. The epic battle between peasants and British soldiers at Avgorou on 5 July 1958, during which a man and a woman were killed and many peasants wounded.

2. The fight between peasants and the Army at Akanthos in December 1957.

3. The fight between women of the village of Spilia and a British detachment on 31 July 1958.

4. In the summer of 1958 a British detachment invaded the village of Agros. The women, having been informed by prearranged signals, gathered in the square where they began to throw stones at the soldiers, who were obliged to beat a retreat to the police station. Later, the British Commissioner of Limassol arrived on the spot, but he too was hit on the head by a stone and compelled to seek refuge in the police station, hotly pursued by the women. The women only broke up after the Commissioner and troops withdrew from the village.

5. The two days' engagement between troops and villagers at Agra and Agridia on 21-22 January 1959.

must be ready to face them, otherwise it is better they should stay quiet. A leader who places himself at the head of such a movement without previously studying the people's capacities is bound to fail. No one ever imagined that the Greeks of Cyprus would be able to hold out against the harsh measures taken then by the British authorities. But nevertheless they did hold out. The Nazis during the last war took the most rigorous measures against the countries in insurrection against them. They even established crematoria in Germany where the inhabitants of the regions in revolt were transported and burnt. Yet the peoples did not yield to force. As regards the deportations, it is not such an easy matter to expel hundreds of thousands or even millions from their homes, because then the question arises of how these people are to be fed.

'Even if one ignores the international organizations which are sure to intervene in such a case – and it is quite possible that the Russians would ignore them – there exists another right, which they are bound to take into account – namely the *right of reprisal*.'

PARTICIPATION OF THE YOUTH. It is among the young people that one finds audacity, the love of taking risks and the thirst for great and difficult achievements. It was to the Youth of Cyprus that I made my main appeal and called on to give their all to the struggle. A youth, which in such a case shows itself indifferent, is a sign of decadence in a country. A country is worth what its youth is worth.

The tasks which I assigned to the youth of Cyprus were the following. Initially, the printing and distribution of proclamations, the rousing of patriotic demonstrations, the collecting of information and the shadowing of suspects. Thanks to their demonstrations, the youth succeeded in misleading and absorbing the attention of large enemy forces, especially in the towns, and at the same time in stirring the feelings of the people whose morale went up when they saw the youth ignore all danger. Subsequently, I assigned young people the task of forming groups of saboteurs, the manufacture of explosives, and the supervision and execution of orders concerning passive resistance. Finally, the youth were a testing ground and nursery from which I selected fighters for my groups of guerrillas and saboteurs. Such was the discipline among the Cyprus youth that it was sufficient for me to give an order for thousands of its members to assemble. The British authorities were compelled again and again to close the schools in many towns for long periods, partly as a punishment and partly to prevent the pupils from holding meetings and discussions in the schools. Yet here again the efforts of the authorities were in vain. The youth of Cyprus endured everything but never yielded, giving a fine example of self-sacrifice and heroism. They have written pages of history of which the Greek Nation will always be proud. The youth demonstrations were of so aggressive a character that they pinned down large numbers of troops, especially in the towns. In order to break them up, the Army often had to make use of its arms, and not a few students were killed or wounded by British bullets.

Schoolboys between the ages of fourteen and seventeen undertook dangerous missions such as the blowing up of aircraft at the British air-bases, the laying of mines and the blowing up of police stations.

I doubt whether there was a single boy above the age of twelve who did not take part in some mission during the Cyprus campaign. I know no other example in history where the whole of a country's youth, boys and girls, has taken so active and effective a part in the struggle for their country's freedom. Even the little boys of the primary schools played their part. Apart from the demonstrations in which they were at the side of their seniors, they carried on a peculiar struggle of their own, the 'Battle of the Flags', as they called it. The British had forbidden the hoisting of the Greek flag on the buildings of Greek primary schools. This is one more example of the psychological ignorance shown by the authorities. They were even naïve enough to proclaim that the Greek flag was a 'foreign' flag, so far as the little Greeks of Cyprus were concerned. This stupid and ill-advised action on the part of the British was exploited by me for the purpose of exciting still further the fanaticism of the young pupils.

It was later that a real fight began. The pupils used to hoist the Greek flag on the school buildings while British soldiers patrolled the villages in order to pull them down. This however exasperated the military because it took up the time of quite a number of troops who would otherwise have been available for operations against our other forces. In time, however, full-grown men also took part in this 'Battle of the Flags', laying a mine below the flag or in some other spot, with the result that the soldier trying to pull down the flag got himself blown up.

The action taken by the British to put a stop to the youth activities, apart from measures of repression, also took the form of preventive measures such as the following. The arrest and holding in detention camps of the most active pupils as well as of a number of teachers who encouraged their pupils in such activities; expulsion of those teachers who came from Greece; permanent or temporary closing of certain schools; and finally – most idiotic of all – the compulsory teaching of English to pupils of the Fifth and Sixth Forms in elementary schools for five hours per week, while reducing the hours devoted to Greek grammar and spelling to only three hours per week. All the above measures, however, failed in their purpose and merely fanned the pupils' fanaticism. (For the manner in which the youth were organized see pp. 26-28.)

ORGANIZATION OF LIAISON. No command can be effective and no victory can be won unless there is a fully organized, properly functioning liaison service.

The small extent of the island and the peculiar conditions of our struggle did not permit of my using any method but messengers for this vital service. A helicopter would have been ideal, but there could be no question of that. We possessed no helicopters, and, even if we had, we could not have used them. Even the use of wireless for internal liaison inside EOKA was not advisable, because in so small an island the points from which a wireless operated would have been easily detected.

At first, our liaison network was extremely primitive, but as the needs of the struggle increased so our network developed and perfected itself.

I was fully aware of the importance of the question as well as of the difficulties which the enemy could place in our way, and so I devoted great effort to organizing our liaison services as efficiently as possible. Throughout the four years that the struggle lasted, thanks to our system, I was never for a moment out of touch with my sectors. A tough fight took place between the British and ourselves over our liaison system, they doing their best to disrupt it and we to keep it going. Again and again we were up against enormous difficulties. The British army in Cyprus had reached the figure of 40,000, i.e. about one British soldier to every ten Greek inhabitants. Every day, on all the roads, the most thorough searches were carried out, even to the complete stripping of men and women, taking car engines to pieces, removing the tyres and all other parts. Any foodstuffs conveyed by road would be scattered on the ground and examined. House-to-house searches were very frequent, and in the streets of towns searches were practically continuous. Despite all these measures, our liaison system was effective, and our losses in the way of correspondence trifling and of small account.

There was a time when I was hiding in a town, practically surrounded by enemy guards. Still our correspondence used to slip through the cordon, through the streets under surveillance, and reach its destination. Great Britain sent out to Cyprus some of the smartest agents of the Intelligence Service (some three hundred of them) including the famous 'Heavenly Twins', with orders to catch Dighenis. They all of them failed and the 'Twins' returned to Britain without having achieved their purpose.

Special measures were taken by me both to hoodwink the British authorities and to ensure that our system of passing information would continue to work in the event of something happening to one of our liaison agents. Thus proclamations in my name were often sent out unsigned, which made the British form all manner of conjectures as to whether I had left Cyprus or else was cut off in some area.

I used a different pseudonym and different way of writing for each sector so that, should the correspondence fall into the hands of the British, they would not be in a position to determine who was the sender. This happened once and the British thought that the correspondence came from 'leading members of the Organization' living in Nicosia where the correspondence was found.

We also took precautions so that, in the event of our liaison network being put out of action, a second reserve network, quite independent of the first, should immediately take its place. Further, the two networks sometimes took over from each other, to lead the enemy astray in case he should succeed, without our knowledge, in getting on the track of the network in operation at the time.

Special security measures, amongst them the following, had been taken with regard to my correspondence. The correspondence reached me by a relay of messengers. The messengers themselves either were not aware for whom the correspondence was destined or else, if they were, did not know my exact residence. Of all the liaison agents employed only one knew where I was staying, and all those with whom he came into contact were given the impression that he too did not know and that I was somewhere far away.

The organization of liaison agents was one of our biggest achievements and contributed decisively to the success of the struggle.

Field-Marshal Harding admitted that EOKA's central command post had at its disposal a skilfully operated postal system, thanks to which Dighenis was personally able to control the actions of his subordinates down to the smallest detail.

PASSIVE RESISTANCE. This was a powerful weapon which reinforced and supplemented the armed struggle. I know of no other case in which this method was used on such a wide scale and with so effective an organization, except in India under Mahatma Gandhi. Unfortunately, few people attach due importance to it – perhaps because they are not in a position to appreciate its value, or because they feel that it demands a big organizational effort and has great difficulties in the way of its success. Consequently they are inclined to neglect it or to do it by halves. In Cyprus passive resistance assumed a special form. Its aim, as I saw it, was to arouse the interest of international public opinion in the Cyprus struggle which would be seen as a well organized movement embracing the whole population. It would show once more the Cypriot people's irrevocable determination to do their utmost to win their freedom.

The methods of passive resistance to which I resorted were economic boycott against the British and administrative boycott to dislocate the machinery of government. The economic boycott was never intended to cause serious damage to the economy of Great Britain, seeing that the trade of Cyprus with the United Kingdom barely represented 0.5 per cent of the latter's total trade. My principal object in organizing the boycott was, first, to make a moral impression on the British people and, second, to create difficulties for the Government of Cyprus by reducing its resources. It is a fact that, as the result of our passive resistance, the Cyprus Government became bankrupt. No longer able to meet its expenditure, it was forced to borrow from the Cyprus banks and from public corporations, besides instituting a government lottery. In addition to these measures, the administration was also forced to impose fresh taxation, for instance on petrol, in order to increase the public revenue. However, we took action against the new taxes with the result that their yield was very small. The Government's losses from the boycott were in the neighbourhood of £10,000,000, a considerable sum for an island of only 550,000 inhabitants. Even in England itself, judging by articles in the British Press, the economic boycott had some effect.

The administrative boycott put the government machinery completely out of gear. For instance, nearly all village mayors and elders resigned, thereby reducing administrative contact between the people and the Government to nil. The civil servants, who had been suitably organized by us, were at our beck and call and could be used, if need be, to strike a final blow at the Government services by going

18

on strike. Besides this, we set up 'Committees of Arbitration' for the settlement of civil disputes and to try criminal cases between Greeks.

All this had the effect of greatly restricting the authority of the British over the people and increased the Organization's prestige. Finally, there was the boycott of British government schools in Cyprus. A striking case was that of the British School at Nicosia where only sixteen pupils took part in the examinations in 1958, as compared with 352 in 1956 and sixty-one in 1957.

Thus passive resistance was completely successful in achieving its aim. All the Cyprus Government could do, in the face of the discipline shown by the Cypriot people and the serious results achieved by passive resistance, was to launch a campaign of personal denigration against Dighenis, and to put forward the plea that the reduction in imports from the Commonwealth meant, in the words of Governor Foot, 'the economic ruin of the island'.

PUBLIC ENLIGHTENMENT and PROPAGANDA. Our aims were: first, to enlighten public opinion, at home and abroad, about the justice of our cause as well as to draw attention to those acts of our opponent which were likely to discredit him internationally; second, to keep morale on the home front at a high level of endurance.

For both the above objectives there were special organs which collected the necessary data, as well as others which disseminated the information in suitable form. I accordingly drew up a general directive for the guidance of the services concerned.

The enlightenment of international public opinion was bound to play an important part in bringing home to all concerned the Cypriot people's demand for self-determination. It is a fact that there were many foreigners and even United Nations representatives who were completely ignorant of why we were demanding our freedom.

Under these circumstances we had a hard fight to wage in the international field against an enemy who unlike ourselves had unlimited resources at his disposal. I should add that I personally, with my very limited means, had to confine my activities to the home front. It was for those who were handling the political and diplomatic side of the question, namely the Greek Government and Archbishop Makarios, to take care of things abroad. Consequently my remarks in this chapter concern only the work of enlightenment and propaganda in Cyprus itself.

Vis-à-vis the enemy we were very much at a disadvantage. The Cyprus Government had on its side:

1. Organized British propaganda, which, in Cyprus, was carried on through the Press, radio and certain persons from England who visited Cyprus pretending to be our friends but, in effect, were agents of the British Government.

2. The Cyprus Government Broadcasting Station and the BBC.

3. The whole of the government machinery and the Turkish element in the island whose fanaticism the administration stirred up against us, as well as the Communists whose support the authorities had enlisted on their side and who did everything in their power to counteract our efforts, both by word and action.

4. Special propaganda leaflets which circulated in hundreds of thousands of copies and were sometimes scattered by air over the whole island.

5. The use of force and bribery through the distribution of abundant funds.

What did we have on our side? Firstly, leaflets which we published and which were circulated all over the island with marvellous success. The Greek Cypriot Press, which was censored and subject to very severe penalties if it published information that might help our cause, was not in a position to help us outright.

As we had no printing press at our disposal, our pamphlets were mimeographed. The service which dealt with the issue and distribution was organized by sectors. Despite the efforts made by the authorities to discover where the pamphlets were printed and attempts to prevent their circulation, and notwithstanding the severe penalties enacted against those who distributed or read them, the pamphlets continued to be issued and circulated freely, thanks to the great care and precaution with which the whole service was organized. It was the young people who undertook the dangerous task of distributing the leaflets, and they carried out their task admirably. Special plans were drawn up to enable our young distributors to escape the attention of the police and soldiers of whom the streets were full. They invariably succeeded in scattering the pamphlets about the streets or delivering them at houses without being caught. The police were obliged to go round the streets picking up the pamphlets under the mocking eyes of the inhabitants.

This pamphlet propaganda must be accounted a major success, when one considers the great efforts made by the authorities to prevent their circulation and their being read by the public, and on the other hand the anxiety of the people who relied on these pamphlets for information on what was going on, and who ignored all the dangers and penalties involved.

Secondly, there was propaganda by word of mouth. This was as effective as the pamphlets. When well organized, a whispering campaign yields first-rate results. But such propaganda had its dangers because it exposed the persons concerned, especially during discussions in closed premises, to being overheard by enemy agents who were lurking everywhere. In our propaganda, whether by pamphlet or word of mouth, we had one valuable advantage which the other side lacked – *truth*. Our opponents, unlike ourselves, used *lies*. The people had ample opportunity of judging between the two and in the end would only believe what we said, never the British propaganda, even on the rare occasions when it did speak the truth. The moral of the fable of the shepherd who always cried 'Wolf!' applies here.

The British, by resorting to all kinds of lies to mislead the people, finally succeeded in persuading them that whatever came from an official source did not correspond to the truth. People's morale cannot be bolstered nor their opinion changed by the use of lies. On the contrary, this has the opposite effect as soon as the truth comes out, as it is bound to do sooner or later. Sometimes it is necessary for the leadership, for reasons of expediency, to conceal an untoward and regrettable event, because of the unfavourable repercussions the news may have – but only for a short time. Sooner or later one must find a suitable opportunity to make the truth known.

This is the only way of winning a people's confidence. Throughout the struggle I never lied to the Cypriot people and that is why they always believed what I said, and followed me in everything. But the enemy too believed in my word. When I proclaimed an armistice, it was accepted as such and while it lasted British soldiers went about without fear, often unarmed, because they knew that I always kept my word. The British, on the contrary, showed again and again that their promises were worthless, and for this reason no one believed them. In this respect, there was a striking difference between our own behaviour and that of the British in Cyprus.

With the very limited but well organized means at my disposal, thanks to the faith and determination which inspired me, I was able to

C

counteract British propaganda, which disposed of unlimited means, and to come out victorious from this further trial of strength.

INTELLIGENCE. Accurate intelligence is a pilot which guides one to the right course of action and brings one to one's objective; it is also a scout which spots traps and rocks which the enemy sets in one's path in the hope of tricking and finally crushing his opponent.

No fight can be carried on without intelligence. Not only must we regulate our movements on the basis of such intelligence and an appraisal of all the data at our disposal, but also when we are preparing to act in a certain way, intelligence that the enemy is taking other action may suggest a different decision or course of action.

To give an instance, on the morning of 11 December 1956, had I not, thanks to thick mist, managed to learn of the presence of a hostile force in the neighbourhood of Spilia, the guerrilla group in that area would have been surrounded and drawn into an unequal struggle. Similarly, if in April 1956 I had not received information about Harding's plan to start large-scale operations against us in the Troodos area, and had I not taken the necessary precautions in time, the results of these operations would have been very different and the outcome of the whole struggle too. I wish to stress that, in the collection of intelligence we were at an enormous disadvantage as compared with the enemy. He had at his disposal the whole machinery of the police, the Army Intelligence Corps, the Intelligence Service itself which included special agents sent out from England. He also made use of other methods – the interrogations to which prisoners were subjected, large funds for bribes, the Turkish population, the Communists, Cypriots serving prison sentences who were allowed to escape and infiltrated our ranks, even Greeks and Turks from Great Britain. One might have expected that with this abundance of means, in so small an island, every movement of ours would have been spotted and every action nipped in the bud, seeing that one was surrounded by enemy agents. Yet nothing of the kind happened. For it is not enough to plant agents everywhere. The important thing is to have a complete and well organized system, carefully directed and controlled, with agents who understand their job. These conditions were not fulfilled on the British side. The organs of the Intelligence Service and the enemy's information services in general acted in a superficial manner which I often had occasion to criticize in my *Memoirs*, quoting specific examples. The majority of the Intelligence Service agents gave the impression of men carrying out not a duty but a troublesome task imposed upon them, and who were above all anxious not to risk their lives. The various paid agents, the Turks, in particular, supplied information which was often false, to justify their pay.

At the beginning of the struggle, the population, through lack of experience, used to chatter in the cafés or elsewhere about what they had seen or heard, thus giving away information to the enemy. I made great efforts to stop this mischief. In the end, the people themselves realized what harm they were doing. From then on they preserved perfect discipline and secrecy. Often members of the same family happened to belong to E O K A without revealing to each other that they were members of the Organization.

My motto was: each fighter should only know what concerned him personally, nothing more. Every member of the public should keep his ears and eyes open but his mouth shut, and tell the Organization of everything that might interest it.

As opposed to the British authorities, we had at our disposal the following sources of information: a small number of agents within the police who kept us informed of both army and police movements; loose-tongued British agents or their servants who in conversation with our own people often gave away important plans or other useful information; an intelligence network among the youth who were always on the look-out for information which they gathered from talking to people or from observation.

Besides the above, the enemy gave himself away either in ostentatious movements and preparations (the bugles used to sound early in the camps whenever some search was about to begin or there was to be an intensive movement of supplies, fuel, etc.) or by bragging. On many occasions we were saved, including myself personally, because the enemy did not take the trouble to conceal his preparations for some coming operation, and not infrequently even the final movements and the main operation itself. Indeed, we often got the impression that the enemy was carrying out manoeuvres rather than actual operations. A contributory factor was the size of the forces employed – often quite unnecessarily. The British failed to grasp the proper tactics they should have used against us, basing themselves merely on a display of strength. The broadcasts and public statements made both by Harding and Foot himself were of a nature which, given my knowledge of their individual character – the former a blunt soldier, the latter a cunning diplomat – enabled me to plumb their thoughts and guess at their intentions.

The information we were able to obtain in the various ways outlined above, however limited, was nevertheless sufficient to enable us to regulate our activities and adopt the necessary security measures from top to bottom of the Organization, so that any move on the part of our opponent should not take us by surprise but rather misfire. This finally proved the safest line of action.

In view of the points I have mentioned, our organization continued to develop throughout the duration of the struggle and to be adapted to the requirements of the moment as well as to the means at our disposal. This was due – and it is worth stressing – firstly, to careful planning (we knew what we had to do and consequently where we should direct our efforts), and, secondly, to the constantly maintained secrecy, to our persistent and systematic operations, but, above all, to the willingness and understanding shown by the population.

SYSTEM OF COMMAND

Many people may be puzzled by our system of command and by the whole way in which we organized our struggle. However, the methods I used were nothing new but were imposed by the facts of the situation. To make my point clear, we should consider the following.

1. All the sections and services which I set up were essential to the execution of the campaign, as laid down in my General Plan and as demanded by the various phases of the struggle. Some of them I did not think of initially. They were suggested to me as the plan developed and was put into practice. Leadership does not lie in foreseeing everything – such a thing would be impossible – but rather in a leader's ability to take in each emergency as it arises, immediately and without hesitation, to see clearly and far ahead, according to his position in the hierarchy of command, and to adapt his original plan to the circumstances by taking the decisions and measures dictated by the new turn of affairs. What is of primary importance is quick decision in carrying out any change of plan.

2. It was impossible for me to command the services of a numerous staff, not even a limited one, partly because I suffered from a lack of able assistants and the best of them had to be employed in command of the units, partly because the presence of a large number of persons in one place would have greatly increased the danger of detection and would have required exceptional precautions for concealment. It

would have been dangerous to establish a Command Group anywhere, of however few members, and enable it to function properly. In the mountains any such group would have been under constant pressure, nor would the liaison with the Organization's other commands have functioned properly. In many cases it would have been cut off for days, even weeks, because of the enemy pressure which was usually particularly intense in the mountain areas.

At first, I set up my headquarters in the mountains among the guerrilla groups, partly to keep up the men's morale, partly to initiate them into guerrilla tactics. During the operations of December 1955 and June 1956, which lasted for many days, I was cut off and closely surrounded, and lost all contact with the sectors. Consequently, I decided to transfer my headquarters to a town where the facilities for liaison were infinitely greater and it would be much easier for me to direct operations. But in a small town with a population of about 30,000 (in Cyprus Nicosia is the only town of 70,000 inhabitants; in the others the population varies from 10,000 to 30,000) it was impossible to have a number of persons hiding in a single or adjacent houses and actively engaged, because their movements and communications were bound to be discovered.

Consequently, I found myself obliged to carry out the duties of Commander and Staff with a single assistant. Naturally, the labour and responsibility involved for the Leader were immense, and it needed great powers of moral resistance to enable one to face, unaided, all the vicissitudes of the struggle for four years. The Cyprus struggle is an example of what can be attained by will-power.

The lack of sufficient experienced assistants compelled me to centralize command though I did my best to diminish the disadvantages attached to such a system.

Had I been eliminated, the whole struggle would have collapsed because no one could have taken my place. Despite its drawbacks, the centralized system of command enabled me to exercise control and maintain discipline over the whole Organization. These were important factors of success. I was, of course, helped by the small extent of the island which enabled me to remain in touch with all the subordinate commands, thanks to our excellent system of liaison.

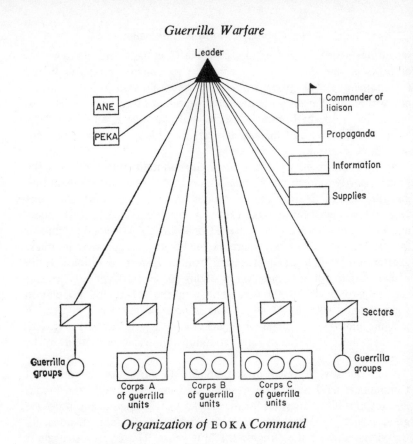

Organization of E O K A *Command*

The diagrams show the organization of E O K A command and the organization of the sectors.

ORGANIZATION OF EOKA COMMMAND

A N E (E O K A Young Stalwarts). This body originated in the towns and gradually the organization was extended over the whole island, till it reached the following form.

A Central A N E Committee was set up at Nicosia. This Committee had no executive powers but acted mainly as an advisory body to the Leader. For the activities of the youth were closely tied up with those of the sectors, with whom they had to co-operate. Consequently, so far as administrative and tactical subordination was concerned, they had to take orders from the chiefs of their sectors.

On the other hand, to secure uniformity in the operation, training

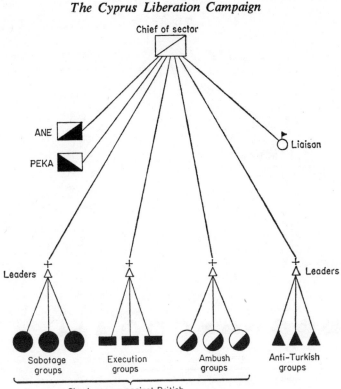

The Cyprus Liberation Campaign

Chief of sector

ANE

PEKA

Liaison

Leaders

Leaders

Sabotage groups

Execution groups

Ambush groups

Anti-Turkish groups

Shock groups against British

Organization of Sector Command

and control of the youth, it was thought necessary to have a single directing body, which took the form of the above-mentioned Central Committee which was directly responsible to the Leader.

Each sector had a Youth Leader who, so far as tactics were concerned, took his instructions from the local sector head, but in matters of organization, training, etc., from the Central Committee. Each sector had three Youth Sections – schoolboys, boys above school age, and girls.

The organization and command of the EOKA Young Stalwarts, with the peculiarity mentioned above which was dictated by the circumstances of the struggle, worked perfectly throughout.

Once more I repeat that, in my opinion, there is no single system or single type of organization which fits a particular case. Usually there are several alternative systems, the best being that which is

27

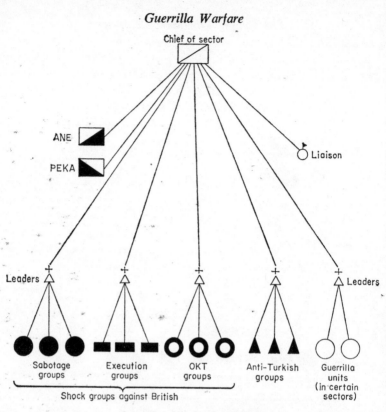

Organization in the Towns

adapted to the general and special needs of each case. Success depends upon the organization being constantly controlled by the local commanders. The E O K A Youth, thus organized and disciplined, played a wholehearted and effective role in the struggle and at the same time remained wholly uninfluenced by Communist propaganda. It is doubtful whether in the course of the struggle a very small percentage, even about 5 per cent, followed the Communist line. Even the children of Communists joined E O K A and remained loyal to the aims of the struggle.

P E K A (Political Committee of the Cypriot Struggle). As early as February 1955, during the secret preparations for the struggle in Cyprus, I issued the first orders for the secret organization of the population. My original aim was to create in each village and town-ward a nucleus of two or three individuals who would gradually

28

multiply by initiating other selected persons, so that they could offer the following services: participation in mass demonstrations in which they would get the remainder of the population in the towns and villages to follow them; provision of hiding-places and shelters for members of the Organization; participation in acts of violence, using arms if necessary; collection and transmission of information; shadowing Government agents.

In each town or village, the individual selected would be divided into categories and drafted, according to each man's ability, into one of the above services. To preserve secrecy and for security reasons, each person was to be acquainted only with the aspect of our activities which concerned him personally and no more. The men belonging to one service should not know who belonged to another even in the same village. In organizing these branches we sought above all *quality* rather than *quantity*.

Later on, when the organization of the sectors was complete and especially from the beginning of 1956 when the total participation of the population began to form part of our plan of action, I made the organization more systematic by establishing the Political Committee of the Cypriot Struggle (P E K A). This body undertook to organize the population, with the following tasks:

1. Co-ordination of the military and civil struggle.
2. Preservation of an unbroken internal front.
3. Raising the morale of the people.
4. Fighting enemy propaganda.

Unfortunately, it was found impossible to constitute a central committee for this body, as I had hoped, because of the difficulty of getting suitable persons. Consequently I decided personally to take over the direction; a solution which was imposed on me by circumstances. In each town or sector we set up a P E K A committee which was subordinate to the chief of the sector. The only exception was Nicosia which for special reasons was independent of the local sector organization and was under my direct personal command. P E K A communicated with the people either by word of mouth or through leaflets and served as the channel through which I made known to the people the Organization's directives and the attitude to be adopted on each question. Later on, when the Turkish danger arose and we decided to launch the passive resistance campaign, I set up a new organization called E A E M (United Unbroken National Front) which had the two tasks of dealing with the Turkish element and organizing passive resistance, under the general guidance of P E K A.

I thought this necessary so as to give the Communists an opportunity of sharing in these two new phases of E O K A's activity, in which their participation was regarded as essential, without letting them into the secrets of the Organization, for obvious security reasons. Unfortunately the Communists, who always adopted a negative attitude towards all our efforts, realizing that they could not hoodwink us and exploit our movement for their own political advantage, not only refused to contribute to our struggle but actively and quite openly opposed our plans for passive resistance. Moreover, in the case of the struggle against the Turks, not only did they refuse to participate, but even in certain cases betrayed members of our organized groups which had been formed for defence against Turkish attacks. Notwithstanding Communist opposition, E A E M worked well and in several rural sectors undertook and brought to a successful conclusion several missions which were within P E K A's scope of activity.

Liaison agents. As regards the organization and functioning of the liaison services, I shall confine myself to the following remarks, for I do not wish to disclose my whole system.

There existed one General Centre, where the correspondence between the Leader and the sectors was centralized. This was responsible for distribution and delivery. For security reasons, the correspondence did not come direct to the Centre but passed through a number of intermediate centres or persons. Thus, in the event of an agent being caught or an intermediate centre discovered, neither the Leader nor the General Centre ran any immediate risk. There was sufficient time to take the necessary precautions. The General Centre was located for security reasons at a distance from the Leader's headquarters and in a different town. This, of course, increased the time needed for communication but had its offsetting advantages so far as regular functioning and safety were concerned. Our transmitting agents were men, women and children who travelled either on foot, in motor vehicles or on pack-animals.

Medical service. We were unable to organize a separate medical service. It would have been very easily discovered and it was out of the question to organize a mobile medical service. Our needs were met as follows. Any of our people who required medical attendance were sent to doctors or clinics in the towns who were affiliated to the organization. The guerrilla units had a first-aid supply and also usually had the services of a trained nurse. In the case of men who were seriously ill or wounded, a doctor went to the spot and gave the necessary instructions for further treatment.

Food supplies and commissariat. These presented no serious difficulties. Our forces that needed supplies were small; moreover, they were all posted in or within easy reach of inhabited places where they could get whatever supplies they required without attracting attention. There was some little difficulty in the case of the guerrilla units. Details of how these were supplied are given on pp. 58-60.

ORGANIZATION OF THE SECTOR COMMAND

Organization in the towns: underground warfare. The organization of Sector Command was not stereotyped but varied with local conditions and needs. In the towns some sectors only had sabotage, execution and ambush groups; others had anti-Turkish groups; others still had their own mountain guerrilla units, as in the Larnaca, Paphos and Solea districts.

The sectors had their own special code of regulations. It was the duty of every sector head to keep his deputy fully informed of everything. But the deputy was precluded from taking an open part in the affairs of the Organization, unless he happened to be wanted by the authorities. This was a precaution against his being detected. Every group in every category possessed its reserves which normally remained inactive to avoid detection, but had to be ready for action at the first call. The members of these reserve units were usually not acquainted with each other, nor, for security reasons, was there any contact between the men of the reserve and those on active service. Thus we were never short of personnel and, except for men who had been discovered and were wanted by the authorities, the rest were unknown persons whose identity was only known to their leaders and who took no overt part in the activities of the Organization.

Town shock groups. At the very start of the struggle, 'shock groups' were organized in the towns. The following tasks were assigned to them: attacks on the police to paralyse their action; harassing tactics against the army by ambushing patrols and attacks on camps; execution of Intelligence Service agents. The weapons the shock groups employed for these purposes were hand weapons and hand grenades.

Later on, however, to counteract the severe measures taken by the British authorities, I carried out a radical reorganization of these groups in February 1957. My principal instructions issued in this connection concerned the careful selection of members and orders for their behaviour in order not to attract attention, and included the organization of a special surveillance service to guard against treachery or indiscretions on the part of members of groups; and the organization in each town of a number of groups, some on active service employed on various missions within the sector, the rest in reserve.

The task of these reserve groups was to undertake individual missions in case of need and to fill gaps in the active groups caused by casualties.

All groups had to be able to carry out any task assigned to them, whether sabotage, executions or other duties, and underwent special training for this purpose. Nevertheless, after the completion of their general training, each group had to specialize, for instance, in executions, ambushes, sabotage, etc. In this way training would be more complete and at the same time there would be a greater degree of efficiency.

The objectives remained the same as before, namely:

1. Military targets, army camps and installations.
2. Ambushing of vehicles.
3. Individual targets (executions).

The struggle within the towns took the form of underground warfare, organized and carried out on a conspiratorial basis.

As soon as the Turkish threat appeared, the system in the towns and sectors underwent certain modifications.

In the towns we set up two combat group corps commands, one directed against the British, the other against the Turks.

The anti-British organization included: execution groups; groups of saboteurs for action against military installations and camps; ambush groups which made use of bombs, electrically-detonated mines, *mikra kanonakia* ('small cannon': see p. 62) and automatic weapons.

The car occupied by General Kendrew and his suite on 9 September 1956 was hit by an electrically-detonated mine. The General had a narrow escape and three of the soldiers accompanying him were wounded.

The anti-Turkish organization included: special units of hand-grenade throwers (ε ο x) under a single leader, trained in the throwing of grenades and street-fighting. These units were quite independent of those for action against the British.

In the villages defence units (ο α) were organized against the Turks. Thus in every sector there existed two corps, one directed against the

British (OKT, sabotage, etc.), the other against the Turks. The second was under separate command to be able to operate independently in case of need. This arrangement was adopted for the greater safety of the respective corps.

GUERRILLA GROUPS

The organization of guerrilla groups. My original plan had been to organize guerrilla units in the Olympus and Pentadactylos mountain areas where the nature of the terrain made it easier to hide or slip away and which, further, were very suitable as a field of operations. Owing, however, to lack of sufficient arms and personnel, I was forced at the beginning to form a few nuclei in the areas of Pitsillia, Lefka and Kalogrea under the best commanders I had at the time. Subsequently, from September 1955 onwards, I also started to organize guerrilla units in the Kykko area on the western slopes of Olympus, so that by the beginning of 1956 I had three main corps of guerrilla units in the following areas: Pitsillia, Kykko (in the Olympus area), Kalogrea (in the Pentadactylos area east of Kyrenia); and one small unit in the Kakopetria area. After staying for a time with the Pitsillia unit whose attacks and engagements against British troops I directed personally, I visited in succession the units in the Kakopetria and Kykko areas which I directed during Harding's large-scale operations in April-June 1956. At the start of the operations the following guerrilla groups were in existence:

Pentadactylos area (Kalogrea-Ayios Amvrosios): strong group of 8-10 men.

Pitsillia area: very well organized group of 8-10 men, under the command of Gregory Afxentiou, who died a hero's death in action.

Kykko mountain area, where I had my headquarters: four groups of 5-6 men in each of the following areas, Vassiliki, Kykkou, Kambos, Tylliria, Milikouri and near Stavros Psokas.

Paphos area: one guerrilla group.

The operations in which these groups took part proved of great and often decisive value to the struggle. For this reason I did my best both to improve their equipment, often at the expense of the towns, and to extend their activities to the lowlands, by organizing a special type of guerrilla unit specially adapted to this kind of terrain, to which I gave the name of OKT (Shotgun Commando Groups: see pp. 69-70). Thus, after reorganizing our guerrilla groups following the casualties we sustained in the ordinary course of events, at the termination of the struggle I had at my disposal the following forces (see also the attached map).

(*a*) Mixed sectors with guerrilla groups

Paphos province	4 units
Larnaca province	3 units
Solea (Evrykou-Kakopetria)	2 units

(*b*) Sectors based on guerrilla groups

Pitsillia	3 units
Spilia	3 units
Phasoula-Paramytha	3 units
W.-N.W. of Limassol (Evdhimou-Kilani)	1 unit
Marathassa (Kykko)	2 units
Tylliria	1 unit

The remaining sectors – namely, Famagusta, Karpassia, Kyrenia, Morphou, Akaki, Dheftera, Kythrea – disposed of a number of units of varying strength belonging to the O K T (Shotgun Commando Groups) which covered all their requirements.

In the above-mentioned mountain areas necessity and the terrain compelled me to organize sectors based on guerrilla groups which I kept under my own absolute control. The leaders of these units also assumed within their zones the duties of chiefs of sector (over A N E, P E K A, E A E M, etc.).

All my efforts were directed towards the creation of a single command of all the guerrilla units, but I came against the difficulty of finding suitable persons. I therefore proceeded by stages. I began by giving Afxentiou the command of the guerrilla groups in the Pitsillia area, with the intention of later on extending his jurisdiction to other areas as well. Afxentiou's death deprived me of this solution and I had to revert to the centralized system under my personal command. Towards the end of the struggle I created the following Combat Group Corps Commands, on Mount Olympus in particular:

Corps A, comprising the 4 guerrilla units in the two sectors of Paphos province.

Corps B, comprising the 3 guerrilla units of Marathassa and Tylliria.

Corps C, comprising the 6 guerrilla units of Pitsillia and Phasoula-Paramytha. The units of the Spilia sector were later to come under this group.

Conclusion. As anybody will realize who studies the organization

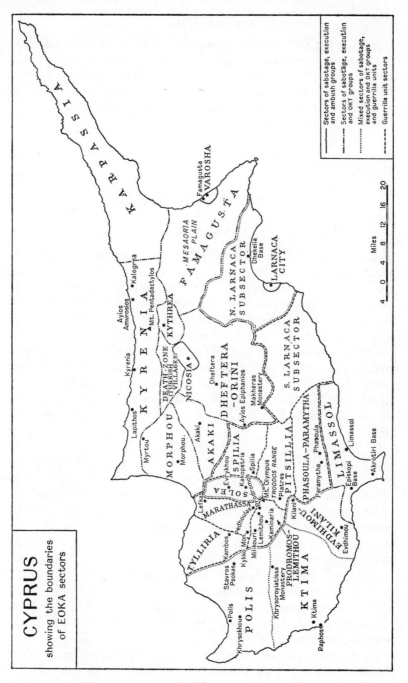

CYPRUS

showing the boundaries
of EOKA sectors

Sectors of sabotage, execution and ambush groups

Sectors of sabotage, execution and OKT groups

Mixed sectors of sabotage, execution and OKT groups and guerrilla units

Guerrilla unit sectors

Miles

0 4 8 12 16 20

KARPASSIA

Famagusta VAROSHA

MESAORIA PLAIN

FAMAGUSTA

Kalograea

Ayios Amvrosios

Mt. Pentadactylos

KYRENIA

KYTHREA

Kyrenia

DEATH ZONE
(TURKISH VILLAGES)

NICOSIA

Dheftera

N. LARNACA SUBSECTOR

Dhekelia Base

LARNACA CITY

Lapithos

MORPHOU

Morphou

DHEFTERA-ORINI

Ayios Epiphanios

Makheras Monastery

S. LARNACA SUBSECTOR

Myrtou

AKAKI

Akaki

SPILIA

Spilia

PHASOULA-PARAMYTHA

Limassol

Lefka

Evrykhou

Kakopetria

Mt. Olympus

TROODOS RANGE

Platres

PITSILLIA

Phasoula

LIMASSOL

Akrotiri Base

SOLEA

Pedhoulas

Korori

Kilani

Paramytha

Episkopi Base

MARATHASSA

Milikouri

Kaminaria

Lemithou

KILANI

EVDHIMOU

TYLLIRIA

Kambos

Kykko Mon.

PRODROMOS-LEMITHOU

Evdhimou

Stavros Psokas

Polis

POLIS

Khrysokhou

Khrysoroyiatissa Monastery

KTIMA

Ktima

Paphos

as given above, I followed no particular 'type' but adapted my organization to our circumstances, modifying it and adapting it continually as time went on. This, of course, is the meaning of 'organization', namely, the most effective use of the means at one's disposal and the co-ordination of those means to yield the maximum results.

4. Strategy and Tactics

STRATEGY

In accordance with the General Plan (see Appendix, pp. 91-95), at first I confined myself to acts of sabotage carried out by the special groups formed for the purpose. Only later on did I start operations with guerrilla bands. I decided to proceed thus, partly because we had not yet formed and trained a sufficient number of guerrilla units, and partly because I did not think it advisable to go all out immediately but rather to wait for the first results of sabotage operations and then, making the decision on the basis of the experience gained, to give priority to that form of the struggle which promised the best results. At the same time, every effort would be made to increase our combat strength so that in time the proper armed struggle might come into being.

By acting thus we achieved the following: Firstly, we took the enemy completely by surprise, thus making him adopt a purely defensive course of action and resort to spasmodic measures based on no planning. Secondly, the police, who had to bear the main brunt of our initial operations, had been almost completely checked. Thirdly, the Army, which was incapable of venturing on any wider field of action requiring initiative, confined itself simply to succouring the police, without however making any concrete plan. Generally speaking, the enemy remained on the defensive and his offensive action mainly took the form of imposing curfews and arresting innocent citizens. Fourthly, we succeeded in gaining the confidence of the people who, apart from sympathizing with our struggle, realized that we were in a position to beat the British forces in Cyprus.

The Commissioner of Larnaca, in a secret dispatch addressed to the Colonial Secretary, dated 28 July 1955, reported that though July had been a quiet month in his province, his information was that it was only a temporary lull and that E O K A was reorganizing its forces and preparing to strike some powerful terrorist blows to coincide with the Tripartite Conference in London.

His report concluded that every precautionary step should be taken before 29 August, and that it was essential not to leave the initiative to the terrorists. The Commissioner added that he was convinced that, whatever steps might be taken by the Government, the present chaotic state of things could not be permanently improved. . . . It was true that severe precautionary measures on the part of the Government would check E O K A's activities and reduce terrorism, but severe measures, however widely applied, would not yield results unless the roots of the trouble were examined.

The Commissioner went on to suggest that the following measures, to be taken at the same time as the precautionary steps proposed by the Commissioners of Famagusta and Nicosia in their despatches to the Colonial Office on the same subject, should be examined:

1. It was essential to take immediate measures to remove the causes of the widespread disaffection among civil servants and to create a government machine which would be 100 per cent loyal.
2. The same applied to the police. The strength of the police was inadequate both from the point of view of personnel and equipment.

The rural populations had lost their confidence in the Government. It was therefore necessary to carry out programmes for the immediate improvement of conditions in the villages in order to recover the people's confidence. Should the Government succeed in winning the rural areas' support, which was quite feasible, then it would be possible to look forward with confidence to the future.

The Government, the Commissioner concluded, should take immediate steps to restore the prestige of the District Commissioners who were its representatives in the provinces and were in a position to exercise great influence in the rural areas. Since a recent report submitted to the Government and the centralized policy subsequently adopted, the prestige of the District Commissioners had fallen in the eyes of the public and the officials. The effect had been to deprive the Government of its sole power of exerting influence in the districts.

The English-language newspaper *The Times of Cyprus*, published in Cyprus, wrote on 4 November 1957:

'Harding as well as the Cabinet in London then believed that E O K A could be beaten with the help of the population. By the time he realized that most Greeks favoured E O K A, it was too late to contrive a more effective policy.

'In a series of farewell speeches the departing Governor has claimed that E O K A can be mastered. He has not, however, claimed that it is mastered.'

The results we achieved, as described above, allowed me on the one hand to proceed actively with the organization of my forces and on the other to increase proportionately my pressure on the enemy.

My tactics consisted in taking the offensive by carrying out surprise attacks with a small number of mobile forces; and in avoiding the enemy's blows and slipping through the available gaps.

MODIFICATION OF THE ORIGINAL GENERAL PLAN

First phase. My original General Plan remained unchanged in its general lines until the arrival of Field-Marshal Harding in October 1955 and his taking over supreme political and military authority in the island. By then the struggle had achieved the first part of its aim – it had aroused the interest of public opinion everywhere.

Although the Tripartite Conference which met in London in June 1955 achieved nothing, nevertheless the Cyprus question began to be seriously discussed in the columns of the British Press and to occupy the attention of the British Government to the extent of their super-seding the Governor of the Island.

Further, the Tenth Session of the General Assembly of the United Nations, before which the question of Cyprus was raised in September 1955, although it did not accept the inscription of the question on the agenda, nevertheless only rejected it by a narrow majority and with many abstentions. This proved that inside this international body the idea was beginning to penetrate that something must be done about the Cyprus question. Consequently, I was faced with a new situation.

Firstly, a soldier was arriving in Cyprus as Governor with instructions and the determination, as he himself stated, to apply a policy of the 'strong hand'. Consequently, we could look forward to a stiff fight against an opponent with greatly increased resources and an able leader in command. Secondly, in so far as the path towards a political solution was ruled out, the struggle was bound to be a long one.

Second phase. As soon as Harding arrived in Cyprus, he proceeded to take preliminary measures for a show-down which comprised the bringing in of reinforcements and a re-deployment of his forces;

manning police posts with military detachments, the Army taking over responsibility for the whole of security; extraordinary measures to guard military installations and camps; the proclamation of a state of emergency throughout the island.

For the first time the Army began to undertake operations in the mountain areas. Harding passed to the offensive. But how did he do it? I certainly did not notice the existence of any comprehensive plan based on a careful study of the situation.

Harding seriously underestimated his opponent whom he took to be a few undisciplined bands of hotheads which could easily be broken up. Consequently, the sum of his strategy and tactics lay, first, in a display of strength, with theatrical military movements such as Cyprus had never witnessed before; second, in terrorizing the population; and third, in launching a silly propaganda campaign against us.

His military activities aimed at imposing, by a display of force, the political views of the British Government, with a view to the political negotiations that had just begun between Harding and Archbishop Makarios. In order to counter Harding's plan I decided not to take the enemy's blows lying down but, despite his enormous superiority, to return them blow for blow in quick succession, and give him not a moment's respite. My principle aim in doing so was to keep up the morale of the people and our fighters. I attached the greatest importance to this for fear of their morale being shaken by the enemy's great display of force. I did detect some signs of weakening among the people, though they were not obviously apparent.

Our General Offensive Plan of Action underwent no changes so far as its basic lines were concerned, only in its execution and methods. This plan was aimed at the following:

1. Preliminary action aiming to create favourable conditions for a new offensive; disrupting the police; wearing down the army; putting out of gear the Intelligence Service's information network.

2. The main action, whose object it was to deal the enemy some vigorous blows.

The execution of this plan demanded that we should hold the greatest possible number of the enemy forces in the maintenance of order in towns and inhabited places, and deliver sudden attacks on these forces in suitable spots, such as ambushes, assaults on camps, etc., thereby causing casualties and lowering enemy morale.

The pinning down of enemy forces was the duty of the youth, through their organizing provocative demonstrations, as well as of a small number of fighters in the towns operating against police and Army forces.

The main action would be undertaken by our principal forces, guerrilla units, sabotage squads and O K T groups.

The action on which we now embarked was well within our capabilities. Our strength had increased, thanks to the reorganization of our forces and the intervention in the struggle of the guerrilla units, whose activities I directed in person, thereby giving them a kind of priority. Moreover, the methods of guerrilla warfare I adopted (which are set out in the section on Tactics: see pp. 47 ff.) allowed me to achieve positive results against an army which was not accustomed to guerrilla methods and always presented mass targets. By acting as I did I attained my objective; for whereas the enemy's losses were considerable and his morale so shaken that on several occasions Harding had to intervene in person to restore it, E O K A ' s prestige and the morale of the people engaged in the fight were higher than ever.

Third phase. In May and June 1956 Harding launched a large-scale offensive with strong forces against our mountain units. It should be noted that Harding, from his first arrival in Cyprus, devoted his main effort to the mountain units to which he obviously attached a major importance. This was the first time that we saw the enemy apply a definite plan. It consisted in covering a wide area with small detachments of men acting independently who carried out searches with the support of helicopters. But if the plan in question at first sight appeared logical, it nevertheless fell flat, owing to the methods used. It was as if the units involved in the operation had warned us by leaving their visiting cards. All their movements were so open that they gave themselves away, and whenever we clashed with them, the behaviour of most of these units and the way they acted was lamentable. For two full months I found myself inside the cordon, but though the enemy had spotted me and surrounded me, I was able again and again to escape capture or death because of the mistakes made both by the detachments themselves and by the enemy commanders at all levels.

It is a moot point whether the enemy should have started with operations against the guerrilla units in the mountain areas, or whether he would have done better to start from the towns and villages. For it was obvious that the guerrilla units were entirely dependent, for supplies and liaison, on the inhabited centres, and if the enemy had succeeded in paralysing all activity and dislocating our organization in those centres, it would have been a serious blow to the very existence of our guerrilla units. It is possible that Harding's idea behind initially starting operations against our units in the mountains is reflected in a report sent by the *Daily Mail*'s correspondent in Cyprus on 1 January 1956, which said that it was far more difficult to deal with the groups in the towns because their members could easily disappear into the crowds or in the labyrinth of streets; it was a much easier task to deal with E O K A's mountain units; since the arrival in Cyprus of large reinforcements these units would certainly have realized that they were bound to be captured as the net was drawn tighter round them.

If the above remarks really reflect Harding's thoughts, then he must have realized later on that he had been wrongly informed and that the guerrilla units were just as tough as those in the towns. In any case Harding had sufficient forces at his disposal to enable him to take simultaneous action against both areas – mountains and inhabited centres – by sectors so as to leave us no breathing space and to keep harassing us on every side.

These operations proved a complete fiasco, both in strategic conception and tactical execution. Barring the capture of a small number of units and individual fighters, they failed to achieve anything against us. Dighenis did not fall into enemy hands, our forces were not completely crushed, the morale of our fighters and of the people was not affected. The best proof of this is that those of our units which had sustained casualties were very quickly reorganized and fresh and stronger units came into being.

Nevertheless Harding, who had gone to London, expected to receive the news of Dighenis' capture any moment, and his staff in Cyprus had even prepared to celebrate their victory by a dinner!

The mistakes made by the British during these operations may be summarized as follows: although they had screened off a very wide area with the disposal of large forces, estimated by me at 8,000-10,000 men, in successive pincer movements, they always left a few gaps through which small groups, with agility, could slip away. If you don't close all the doors in your house, you might as well close none of them. Thus, although surrounded together with my Command Group, I again and again managed to slip through the gaps in the enemy's cordon for twelve whole days, and finally was able to effect my escape, taking refuge and getting food and information in the villages and monasteries over which the enemy kept no proper guard. Besides committing this mistake, instead of sending reconnaissance parties into the surrounded area to comb the ground thoroughly and go over the whole terrain like bloodhounds, all they did was to send a very small number of parties along certain trails in the hope that they would force us either to perish from hunger or surrender. They were obviously unaware that we were determined and well prepared not to submit to either fate, seeing that we were plentifully supplied with food and were always on the look out for a way to slip through as part of our regular tactics.

Our opponent used neither surprise nor secrecy in his movements which were always visible. We were often guided by the enemy's movements in deciding on our own actions. Our tactics were those of the cat which hides and then suddenly pounces on its prey.

For several days they continued carefully to search the area where I and my Command Group had had an encounter with a British patrol, and never extended their search in a circular movement beyond the zone, to anticipate the possibility of a break-through.

The inhabited areas within the zone of operations were negligently guarded. To take an example, just as we were entering the village of Kaminaria on the evening of 11 June 1956, the Army was moving out. After we had provided ourselves with food and received information, we retired from the area on the evening of the next day just as the troops were moving in again. The police dogs they had with them were not only inadequately trained but also incapable of taking up the scent. On the night of 6-7 June the barking of a dog belonging to a military detachment quite close to our hiding-place, gave us warning and enabled us to escape.

The roads inside the zone of operations remained almost totally free from search and were not used to keep track of our movements, although we were often compelled to cross them without being noticed. Yet it was much easier to keep these roads under surveillance, owing to the better visibility and the possibility of using fast vehicles, and it should have been done, seeing that any party surrounded would be obliged to cross one of these roads in order to pass from one zone into the other.

Fourth phase. But as the enemy gradually improved upon his plan of action and adopted new methods we too had to change our plans. The factors on which I had to base my new dispositions were the following.

The enemy, greatly reinforced and always extending his activities, offered us important targets both in towns and in rural areas. On our side, the morale both of civilians and combatants was very high, thanks to our successes. The whole of the population was on our side. Our material resources in arms and equipment had considerably increased, particularly in explosives and sabotage contrivances, in fact to such an extent that we were now self-sufficient. This factor combined with the willingness of the population made it possible for us to increase our forces so as to form a substantial nucleus in every village.

With these considerations in mind I drew up the following plan: *to transform the whole island into a field of battle so that the enemy should not feel secure anywhere*; and to give him the impression that we were *everywhere*, without his being able to detect us or else only exposing to him unimportant targets. The enemy would thus have the feeling that the field of battle was a vacuum.

The tactics to be employed would consist in surprise attacks by small units which would then slip away and vanish. They would fight on the ground and then take cover, either above ground or below. In other words, a type of warfare which would inflict casualties, wear down and exasperate the enemy, was our main objective.

But there were also certain imponderable factors on which I relied and which entered into my calculations, both from the strategic and tactical point of view.

The moral factor. Our struggle, like any other struggle, was mainly a tussle of wills, in which the upper hand would be gained by the one whose moral stamina was higher and his will stronger. I always reckoned on this factor. Throughout the struggle I succeeded in keeping up the morale both of combatants and non-combatants at a very high level. There was never any sign of yielding. An important contributory factor was of course faith in the justice of our cause, whereas the British soldier on the contrary was well aware that he was fighting in order to keep a people in subjection. Thus it was that the ranks of our fighters, even when depleted by casualties or when hard hit, remained unbroken and were quickly reconstituted, with increased cohesion.

Surprise attacks – stratagem and ruse. All these enabled us to neutralize the enemy's superiority in numbers.

The execution of my plan on the above basis continued until the very end of the struggle, in its main lines, and differed only in the methods used, with excellent results.

Fifth phase. Towards the middle of 1957 a new threat appeared in the offing – co-operation between Turks and British. As soon as I realized that the British were encouraging the Turks to attack us and were even going so far as to supply them with arms, I was forced to take this new threat with all due seriousness.

Consequently, after careful study, about the middle of 1957 I drew up plans for warding off Turkish attacks in towns and villages and issued detailed orders for the means and methods to be adopted.

Thus, when at midnight on 7 June 1958, a howling Turkish mob, under the very eyes and protection of the British authorities, launched an attack on the inhabitants of the capital Nicosia, and such attacks soon spread all over the island, they did not find me unprepared.

These unprovoked attacks on the part of the Turks went through two main phases, in two different forms. The first phase comprised attacks of Turkish mobs on Greek quarters in the towns. From the military point of view, the aim of such attacks was, first, to neutralize all resistance on the part of the Greek population in order to force the latter to accept the new British partnership scheme and thus isolate E O K A by the withdrawal of all support; and, second, to force us to fight on two fronts in Cyprus, against both British and Turks.

From the political point of view, the aim was, first, to underline and reinforce the argument invoked by the British that Turks and Greeks could not coexist in the island and prove it correct, and, second, to stir up Turkish intransigence as a means of proving the British Government's inability to satisfy the Greek claims.

The rapidity with which we acted, the excellent preparation and immediate execution of the plan which was already complete in every detail and, above all, the courage and self-sacrifice of all the Cypriot Greeks bore their fruit.

At first we stood on the defensive against both Turks and British. Naturally, we did not wish to get involved at once in a fight on two fronts. I wanted to economize on time and forces. Time was essential to enable me to adapt my dispositions to both present and future conditions, in the event of a change of tactics on the part of the Turks.

I also had to economize my forces and keep my reserves intact to be able to cope with the British should they launch a large-scale operation against us.

Later on, after settling scores with the Turks, I would again go on the offensive against the British whom I had always looked upon as our principal and most dangerous opponent.

After the isolated attacks of the Turks had failed to produce the expected results, there began the second phase – that of out-and-out Turco-British co-operation. The Turkish attacks were now directed against everything Greek, whether persons or property. Individuals were murdered, Greek houses and shops set on fire, municipal buildings seized, Greeks living inside the Turkish quarters expelled from their houses which were then occupied by Turks. The loss of human life was considerable. All this happened under the very eyes and with the connivance of the British authorities.

My plan of action in the face of this second phase of Turco-British co-operation was first to check the Turco-British attacks and subsequently to mount a small-scale offensive against the Turks in order to damp their morale and raise that of our own people, but without wearing down my own forces. Having attained these objectives I would at the proper moment launch a counter-offensive against the British, while at the same time holding down the Turks.

My action against the British was dictated by the following considerations: first, not to leave the British unmolested. It would have been a great mistake to allow myself to be drawn into a wearing struggle against the Turks, leaving the British to play the part of simple spectators. That would have been to play the British game.

Second, not to wear out my forces in order to enable us to hold out for a long time. Consequently, we should not let ourselves be drawn into extended operations. Our activity should therefore be confined to small-scale and sporadic acts of sabotage against installations in order to confuse and exasperate the British; executions of individual Englishmen, first on a small and later on a more extended scale; surprise attacks against armed forces.

I was careful to keep in my own hands the determining of the intensity and duration of each operation.

About the middle of July 1958, after plenty of preparation, I launched a counter-offensive against the Turks, having received information that their morale was at a low ebb and that their activities were on the decrease rather than the contrary because of the strong and persistent resistance put up on our side which they had not expected. Towards the end of July 1958 I also went on the counter-offensive against the British. Both counter-offensives however were kept within the strict limits imposed in rural areas by the nature of guerrilla warfare and in towns by that of underground conspiratorial activity.

The Turco-British alliance and attacks failed and produced the opposite results to those expected in responsible British quarters.

The first to call for an end to bloodshed was Foot, the man who had provoked the Turkish attack, and he was followed by Macmillan himself and the Turkish Prime Minister, Menderes.

The international repercussions, particularly in Great Britain, were serious. The tortuous aims pursued by the British Government were exposed, together with their inability to impose their rule on Cyprus. A section of the British Press began to talk about a 'tragic failure' in Cyprus. On the other hand, the moral repercussions among the Greeks fighting in Cyprus were immense. The Organization's prestige rose and the struggle continued with morale undiminished and increased hopes of ultimate success.

The difference between our strategy and that of the British was striking. One can describe it by the following simile: the British were hunting field-mice with armoured cars. But one can only catch mice with cunning, and the means one must employ are cats and traps. In the case in point, instead of ostentatious Army and Air Force operations, it would have been much better to have organized small 'man-hunting' parties, continually on the move, and capable of putting up the game from its hiding-place, just as a sportsman uses his dog to discover and start the quarry. It is true that the British published the news that they had brought in anti-guerrilla specialists from the Colonies, but I never came across them and I never heard anything of their activities.

Instead, the British flooded Cyprus with troops, so that one met a soldier at every step, with the only result that they offered plenty of targets and so sustained casualties. They completely ignored the principle of 'saturation' of the terrain. In accordance with this principle, each separate kind of terrain has a limit to its capacity of absorption of means without risk. Beyond this limit, any increase in forces not only does not yield better results but, on the contrary, increases casualties and complicates movements to the extent of placing the operation itself in jeopardy. In a secret document emanating from Police Headquarters at Famagusta, dated 24 September 1956, it is specifically stated:

'The application of massive force will only suppress terrorism and drive it further underground. The only way to succeed in eradicating terrorism of the Cyprus pattern is to play them at their own cat and mouse game. This calls for ingenuity tempered with stealth and cunning, except that we must adhere to our own code of "Queensberry Rules", which E O K A, of course, don't have to observe. We must absolve this disadvantage by even greater cunning and resolution.'

What could be more reasonable, simple and plain? The astonishing thing is that neither Harding nor those who succeeded him in command of the armed forces in Cyprus paid any attention to this wise and realistic advice. It is quite possible, however, that the British commanders did see how they ought to act but in practice were unable to follow this advice, because they were carried away either by events or by the sense of their own overwhelming material strength; for there is a great difference between theory and practice.

In various studies and handbooks on guerrilla warfare, mention is made of 'fast-moving, mobile units' etc. for use in operations against guerrillas, whereas in my opinion what is needed is a special organization of specialized forces corresponding to the general and special conditions of the struggle.

TACTICS

OUR TACTICS AND THOSE OF THE BRITISH

The methods we used were surprise, stratagem and ruse, and our tactics consisted in dealing the enemy hard and carefully prepared blows of small duration, followed by rapid disengagement and a period of complete tranquillity in the area. According to circumstances, an operation was either personally directed by me or left to the initiative of the local sector chief.

In the former case, I took over personal command when some wider result was aimed at, in which case the targets were chosen and studied beforehand. The role of the E O K A High Command consisted in co-ordinating the activities of all the branches – guerrilla units, execution, sabotage and O K T groups – both as regards time and place, within the limits of our general strategy and tactics. Our aim was to inflict casualties, wear the enemy down and cause confusion in his ranks.

In the latter case, it was left to the sector leader's initiative to choose both target and time of action, and the targets chosen were any that might turn up.

The above two systems were resorted to turn by turn. The choice of this or that method, or the decision for an interlude of inaction, during a temporary suspension of hostilities, were often dictated, especially in the last instance, by political reasons – diplomatic negotiations, the need to comply with some resolution of the United Nations, and so on. The reader will find the various methods set forth in the relevant section (pp. 57 ff.). I would stress once more that these methods did not remain unchanged throughout the struggle but were subject to constant modification according to circumstances. The increase in our material strength as well as the addition of fresh resources made it possible to adopt new methods of combat. Furthermore, a change of method became necessary as soon as the enemy had familiarized himself with those previously used and was therefore able to react more effectively. Seeing that I was always very much at a disadvantage *vis-à-vis* the enemy from the point of view of resources, I tried to make up for this disparity through better use of the element of surprise.

Our constant change of tactics and methods worried the enemy. The British, depending as they did on so clumsy and cumbrous a weapon as their army in their efforts to counter our invisible units, were not in a position to react effectively. Mostly they had to stand on the defensive because their tactics were merely a response to ours. At all events I never noticed the existence of any over-all offensive plan such as might have led to the annihilation of our units.

After the beginning of 1957 the British began to adopt various methods for tracking down our units such as the following. In areas suspected of harbouring guerrillas, patrols were sent out on foot or in motor vehicles in the hopes of provoking an attack. If the patrols were attacked, they informed their command by wireless and the area was then screened off.

On other occasions, there would be a daily movement of motor transport in such areas and men would be dropped in isolated spots so as not to attract attention. The vehicles would move away giving the impression that they were withdrawing their troops from the area, while the men left behind would form into groups and start a search of the suspected points. In the evening the vehicles would return and take away the men. Occasionally a few would remain in ambush.

Sentinels with field-glasses would be posted on the heights so as to keep an eye on dangerous and suspected areas.

Permanent garrisons would be installed in villages adjoining wooded areas to prevent the guerrillas from obtaining food supplies. At night these garrisons would watch the paths and roads leading from the villages to the surrounding forests.

When a wide area was being searched, a radio announcement would be broadcast that such and such a region was being searched while actually the search would extend over a much wider area than the one indicated.

During extensive operations of this nature, when the enemy was without exact information as to the whereabouts of our units, he would surround a large area and station some of his troops in ambush. The main body of his forces would then invade the area to be combed and would move towards certain points where they would scatter over the whole area with the aid of helicopters. After this, if any particular area aroused suspicion it was kept under continual helicopter observation pending the transfer of troops to the spot.

One cannot, of course, criticize these methods, but every method can be countered. Further, its success depends on the way it is carried out. In war everything depends on the manner of execution. I can mention instances when detachments of troops, engaged on the search of an area, passed quite close to our hiding-places, searching in a wholly perfunctory way, as if they could not be bothered; or they would carry out an operation so openly and in so lackadaisical a manner that one got the impression they were merely engaged on an exercise.

To such methods as these we would react as follows: During the day we would lie low without moving. In the event of our having to move, we would use concealed ground or move under cover of night, but in any case never by the roads or paths. We never lit fires. For a full twelve days during which with my Command Group I was trying to escape from the clutches of strong forces which had surrounded me, I chose to pass over very rough, precipitous ground rather than use roads or paths, and whenever I had to cross a road I only did so after careful reconnaissance, taking every precaution and moving with the utmost speed. The enemy detachments, by carrying out their activities in so perfunctory and open a manner, constituted our principal targets and we lay in wait for them at certain chosen points suitable for ambush.

A British journalist, who visited Cyprus in mid July 1957, described the new tactics adopted about that time by the British against our units in the following terms:

'Groups composed of six men, with wireless, one police dog and a second dog trained in spotting mines, are dispatched by helicopter to areas where suspected persons make their appearance. These groups are supported by a commando. Ambushes will also be set at the approaches to villages in the Troodos and Paphos districts.'

He went on to admit that the EOKA bands made full use of the natural advantages of the terrain, that they received help from the villagers and were tough, adroit and plucky. This tribute is an acknowledgement that our bands possessed all the qualities required for guerrilla warfare.

In towns and rural districts where we were active the enemy relied on patrols as is shown by an order emanating from Divisional Police Headquarters, Famagusta, dated September 1956, which fell into our hands, specifying:

In towns
1. Foot patrols at fixed points
2. Mobile patrols in wireless cars
3. Q Patrols

In rural areas
1. Foot patrols in the villages
2. Motor-cycle and bicycle patrols between outlying villages
3. Military type ambush patrols

Q Patrols. These belonged to a special body composed of British Special Branch and Turkish police, in plain clothes, using private cars. The principal aim of these patrols was to surprise and catch members of EOKA belonging to our bomb-throwing parties before they could carry out their job, and, secondarily, to keep the members of EOKA in a state of uncertainty as regards the intentions of the British forces.

These Q Patrols were regarded as the most important body in the Special Branch which was commanded by Police Inspector Forside. The idea behind them was that military vehicles, equipped with wireless and manned by policemen in uniform, would not only be recognized by members of EOKA but would also offer an easy target for bomb attack. The Q Patrols, as seen by the British, 'introduced the element of surprise against EOKA, i.e. the latter was hoist with its own petard'. The aim behind the use of these patrols was 'to facilitate the taking of initiative at the right moment'.

Their method of operation was as follows: two cars were detailed to patrol a certain sector of the town, keeping at some distance from each other. At an agreed signal they would block a busy section of the street, the men would jump down and start a quick search of the male inhabitants and vehicles. The search party, as it began its work, was covered by a second group. They might use supplementary patrols of plain-clothes policemen mounted on bicycles, who worked in pairs inside the same sector and who by mixing among the crowd were in a better position to spot suspects. They worked on a co-ordinated plan after all those taking part in the operation had been carefully coached. The same methods could be applied with cars and motor-cycles operating in pairs, especially when quick action was necessary.

Mobile patrols. Each quarter of a town was supervised by a police force consisting of one or more police officers in uniform and four or more policemen (the strength could be varied according to circumstances) and supplied with a wireless. One section of the force was employed in mobile patrols which were engaged on controls and searches. Some members of the force could be transported by car to any spot where an incident had taken place or could answer any summons by wireless.

These patrols also had at their disposal a certain number of reserve cars for carrying out normal independent duties, especially on the outskirts of towns. The British were convinced that the use of parties of police, in combination with other plain-clothes patrols, would prove a highly effective weapon against the terrorists. Undoubtedly, taken as a plan, logically worked out in every detail, it could not fail to have some success and cause us difficulties. Nevertheless, it was not able to neutralize our activities. For the system had several weak points and lacunae which made it possible for a resourceful opponent to escape being caught in the net. I do not propose to reveal what these weak points were or how our men nearly always succeeded in giving these patrols the slip, nor to disclose how our correspondence used to slip through. I will only say this, that our men, when they undertook a mission, did so only after careful reconnaissance and preparation, and it was these patrols which provided us with our best targets.

Further, these patrols never prevented EOKA fighters from executing isolated British agents right under their very noses. Consequently, some other more effective system was needed to put an end to our activities in the towns, especially in ones as small as those in Cyprus which averaged 15,000 to 30,000 inhabitants, with the single exception of Nicosia with some 70,000. It is true that the police system in the towns from time to time underwent improvements, but these were of a superficial nature. What was needed was not merely an improvement but a change of system.

Rural patrols. The purpose of these was to surprise members of our Organization lying in ambush by means of counter-ambushes and to unearth those of our fighters hiding in the villages in order to prevent them from operating outside. Admittedly, this system of counter-ambushes was excellent and sometimes yielded good results. It was the only one of which we took some account. We always stood in fear of the 'lurking cat'. One cannot understand why the British later preferred to use other systems involving a great display of force, the invasion of villages by troops supported by helicopters – methods which sent the mice scurrying into their holes.

Later on, the British themselves adopted guerrilla tactics of a kind, with the sudden penetration of small forces into areas regarded as centres of our activity. But this method too could not be effective – a mere invasion of cats into an area is not sufficient to exterminate the mice. The latter merely go into hiding in their nests and wait. It is only by constantly being alert and maintaining great stealth that the cats will be able to spot the mice and catch them at the moment when they emerge.

In order to discover the hiding-place of our members whom they were trying to capture they used army tracker dogs, but to no effect. The victims of these dogs were usually innocent civilians. In one case a dog, on the trail of one of our saboteurs, ended up in the house of an old woman to which he was led by the smell of the blood of a slaughtered hen. Sometimes these same dogs would make straight for houses where there were bitches. In another case a dog led a party of soldiers to a rabbit warren which the soldiers took for an ammunition cache. I myself remained for five full hours surrounded by British troops, while their dog was wandering round the bushes in which I was hiding without ever detecting me. Against these dogs the most effective weapons were garlic and pepper. The scent of both these renders the dogs incapable of following up the tracks of their quarry and even destroys their sense of smell for good. To blockade villages or areas, especially during a search for wanted persons, the British used helicopters in combination with infantry. A number of helicopters would fly low over the whole village area while another helicopter landed inside the village to proclaim a curfew.

Subsequently, applying the principle of constant change of method which, as I have already said, was an important element in enabling me to surprise and confuse the enemy, I made extensive use of percussion mines as well as of organized mass resistance on the part of the population.

The surprise proved so complete that for some time the enemy sustained our blows without any means of reacting effectively. To counter our new methods the British resorted to new tactics.

To avoid our ambushes, they limited the circulation of military vehicles to daytime, because by day counter-action was easier. So supply convoys were escorted by planes and in the event of an ambush reinforcements were quickly summoned and transported to the spot by helicopter and car. But when a vehicle had struck a mine all that the reinforcements found on arrival were the fragments of the mine.

As a measure against the danger from mines, the British resorted to taking hostages. They would arrest innocent civilians in the villages and put them on their vehicles, reckoning that we would not attack them for fear of injuring our own people. We reacted to this by letting loose hordes of women who assaulted the soldiers and often compelled them to release their hostages.

At night the enemy would lie in ambush along roads and paths, and especially near springs where they suspected we drank. In addition, they did not abandon their previous tactics of operations on a wide scale with large forces, which, besides the impression they created, would, they thought, prevent us reorganizing and cause us casualties. But these large-scale demonstrations failed in their purpose, partly because our units slipped away and went into hiding, partly because these operations did not cover the whole of the island and were not continuous but succeeded one another at intervals and in different areas. Thus they in no way hampered our reorganization, while our casualties were replaced just as soon as calm was restored in the area.

In the field of psychological warfare, the British used propaganda, slander, intimidation of the civil population, curfews, etc.

Towards the end of the struggle the new commander of the British forces, General Darling, proclaimed with a great flourish of trumpets that he had put new tactics into practice. These, as far as I could see, consisted in the blockade of whole areas with a wide use of helicopters and light aircraft; in keeping the people in a constant state of nerves by frequent patrols in towns and villages; and in abandoning the policy of blockading and searching villages and harassing the population. Instead, he used a number of tricks intended to deceive our people.

For instance, a British soldier, his face and clothes dyed red to give the impression that he was wounded, would be left near a village or a road regarded as dangerous for traffic. His rifle would be left lying by him, and soldiers would be hiding in ambush a short distance away – all this in the hope of decoying our people.

Again, one or two soldiers armed only with revolvers would enter a village and walk about while a party of soldiers would lie in wait close by. In this way they hoped that our men would give themselves away by attacking the soldiers who had entered the village.

Soldiers mounted on donkeys were also used as decoys to draw our groups. These soldiers would proceed some distance ahead, followed by a small force. The idea was that our men, spotting an isolated soldier riding a donkey, would attack him. Or else soldiers with a knowledge of Greek and wearing baggy Cypriot trousers or disguised as gipsies, would pretend they were members of our Organization and ask for lodging and food. Any person volunteering to provide these was at once arrested.

Needless to say, General Darling's new tactics had no effect upon us – there was nothing very new about them, and his baited traps did not deceive the shrewd Greek Cypriots.

Thus, by constantly changing our methods and making use of the one best adapted to the needs of the moment, we succeeded in taking on, first, the British and, subsequently, British, Turks and Communists combined.

For each of these opponents, though they worked together, I applied special tactics.

Against the British, who had troops at their disposal, my tactics consisted in dealing them blows, whenever they made their appearance and provided targets open to successful surprise attack.

The Turks operated under the protection and guidance of the British, either by conspiracy or in gangs which were let loose, especially in the towns, against Greek-inhabited quarters and Greek citizens, murdering, looting and destroying beneath the passive eyes of the British forces. Against their underground operations my orders were to retaliate in kind. Our defence against Turkish attacks in villages and towns took the following form: in the event of mass action by a Turkish mob, I had a special plan for each town providing for the organization of self-defence by the population (see Appendix pp. 96-98). This consisted mainly in occupying points of vantage along the route to be followed by a Turkish mob and attacking them with firearms or bombs, especially the latter. At first we chose positions at windows or on roof-tops. But this proved to be a disadvantage because our men were hemmed in there and were arrested by the British if there was no way of escape. Cyprus towns have no buildings of many storeys or large adjacent blocks which could be defended for a long time. To hide or escape from house to house was no easy matter. But if men took up their position along the street or nearby, this too had the disadvantage that they might be arrested with arms in their hands before having a chance to fire. Consequently, we used both methods according to the opportunities that each station provided for our men to get away with their arms. For the execution of this plan we had special groups, independent of those organized for the struggle against the British and under separate command.

The defence of the villages was organized in accordance with a general order issued by me (see Appendix pp. 98-99 ff.). In the event of a village being attacked men from the neighbouring villages would come to its aid, and reprisals would be taken against wholly Turkish villages.

To avoid casualties or discovery, our guerrilla groups were to be employed against the Turks only on a very limited scale. We suspected that the British, who feared our groups' activities when directed against their own forces, would probably use the Turks to draw out the guerrillas into areas where they could then be annihilated. My orders consequently were that our units were only to intervene after careful consideration of the circumstances, more especially for the taking of reprisals against Turkish villages. In such cases, the action undertaken should be of short duration after which they should disappear as quickly as possible.

Finally, there was an additional danger from the so-called 'security forces', namely the Turkish auxiliary police who formed a separate corps. The members of this auxiliary force would be let loose at night and during curfew hours to burn and plunder shops at their leisure. Other members of this force, dressed in plain clothes, would carry out murderous attacks on persons in Greek cafés or houses.

It is obvious that defence against the Turks created a number of problems for us, for quite apart from the casualties we sustained and the effect on the morale of the Greek population, there were many tactical problems we had to face.

Thus, whereas Turkish gangs would attack Greek quarters under British protection, the Greek inhabitants, when they hit back, were chased away from their stations by the British. If they attempted a counter-attack the British would check up, and any person found holding a club, stone or other defensive weapon, would be arrested. Through the Turks the British often tried to create a situation in villages or towns which would give them an opportunity to see our reaction and arrest some of our people while carrying arms.

Consequently, strict orders were issued to our men instructing them how to behave and what use to make of their arms. The Greek Cypriot fighter, thanks to his intelligence and pluck, very soon succeeded in adapting himself to the new situation and when counter-attacking against the Turks was careful to avoid pursuit by the Turks' British allies.

It was no mean achievement for a small and unarmed people to stand up to powerful opponents inside small towns and villages and carry on a victorious struggle which can be compared to fighting in an enclosed open space.

The action taken by the Communists against us lay mainly in their coming to secret terms with the British and showed itself in the betrayal of some of our members and in our being opposed whenever we took up a public stand against the British political plans. The tactics I used against the Communists were, firstly, encirclement and a close watch to prevent them from taking armed action, even if they received arms from the British or abroad, and, secondly, intimidation by the execution of those convicted of betraying our members. To have been able to wage a successful fight simultaneously against three powerful opponents with the very slender means at our disposal is an almost incredible achievement. It was due both to the devotion and determination of our immediate counter-attacks against all our opponents, a course of action which kept up the morale of the people; and, also, to the use of elastic tactics, as dictated by the circumstances, against each one of our opponents. A leader who has to deal with a certain situation must, after careful study, apply the appropriate tactics. He should not stick to hard-and-fast rules but should show inventiveness and initiative.

The success of our strategy and tactics was admitted even by our opponents. Thus Field-Marshal Montgomery said that, strategically,

EOKA was invincible. The London *Observer* wrote that the civil and military authorities in Cyprus acknowledged that EOKA could not be crushed. The London *Daily Herald* admitted that one field-marshal, three generals and 40,000 British soldiers had failed to conquer EOKA.

FURTHER ORGANIZATION AND METHODS OF COMBAT

GUERRILLA UNITS. *Organization and choice of means.* In Cyprus there were no men with war experience or even trained in the use of arms. Consequently, the organization of the units, the training of the men, their first action and the extent of that action had to be regulated by stages.

At first I selected members from the regions where they would operate. But my most difficult task was the men's tactical training which had to take place under the noses of the British. I started by theoretical instruction, followed by skirmishes with the police, and completed their training by engagements with British forces. Thus these units were taught how to fight by actual combat. I did my best to bring off our first clashes successfully in order to raise the men's morale. To achieve this I did not hesitate to place myself at the head of the strongest guerrilla unit and take part in the fighting so as to set an example and show the men how to operate. After that, for about a year, I went round nearly all the units in succession and stayed with them some time. In time these units acquired a lot of experience so that, although small in number, they managed to keep on the move and occupy the attention of the greater part of the British forces in Cyprus, without the latter ever succeeding in inflicting a decisive blow; whereas our people caused the enemy substantial casualties.

I went to great trouble in selecting my guerrillas, for it is not everyone who has the aptitude for such a task. The guerrilla must be the perfect type of fighter and should possess certain qualities in a greater degree than even the best ordinary soldier for he will have to fight under infinitely more difficult conditions. The guerrilla has to struggle against solitude, the isolation which surrounds him, the lack of all assistance and often the lack of comrades; he will find himself in circumstances which will necessitate his taking decisions, sometimes very bold ones, alone; he may have to go without food and water for days on end; he will have to march continuously day and night, sometimes for long periods, in order to avoid the danger of being hemmed in by the enemy; he will have to carry on his shoulders food, arms, bedding and all other necessities. Given the conditions under which he is called upon to live and operate, he must possess the highest degree the qualities of boldness, resourcefulness, cunning, initiative, optimism, a strong constitution, sobriety and resistance to hardships, hunger and thirst, etc. A guerrilla unit is a kind of moving family which carries with it all its requirements for sleep and food. The Greek, who is by nature frugal and self-sufficient, easily adapts himself to such a life. Pulse, a few olives, cheese and tinned food may be his daily diet for weeks.

The age of our guerrillas varied between 17-18 and 30-35 years. But we also had some who were over 50 and who did very well. Dighenis himself was over 58 years old at the time when he was climbing the mountains of Cyprus and fighting with his guerrillas.

Strength, hide-outs and food supplies of guerrilla units. The strength of each group varied from four to five men. The experience acquired during the struggle showed that a larger number was not only unnecessary but could be harmful. The missions undertaken by such units could be carried out by a small number of men, whereas, whenever we attempted to form bands of eight to ten men, they proved less mobile and secure, besides the difficulty of keeping them supplied with provisions. When a larger force was needed for an operation, two or more units would temporarily combine or be reinforced by the Shotgun Commando Groups. Once their mission was accomplished, they would break up again. To avoid misunderstandings and confusion, each unit had its own zone within which it moved, operated and drew its supplies. Each unit had its lair, usually a hide-out dug in the ground, with supplies for several days, so as to be in a position to hold out if surrounded or cut off from its bases of supply. Usually each unit had more than one such hide-out so it could move whenever that hitherto occupied proved unsuitable. These places were carefully selected, the requirements being safety and facility of escape. The hide-outs proved most useful and extremely difficult to discover. In most cases the enemy only got to find one through betrayal. In two cases hide-outs were spotted through the marks of footsteps on the surrounding muddy soil. Consequently, I recommend making hide-outs on rocky soil and on mountain slopes of difficult approach. The entrance to ours was a hole through which only one man could crawl at a time. It was well closed and camouflaged to render discovery very difficult for anyone not aware of its existence. In most cases we avoided using inhabited places for our hide-outs because we suffered a good many losses either through inability to conceal the movements of those hiding there or else as the result of an indiscretion on the part of the inhabitants or carelessness on the part of liaisons or purveyors of supplies, whose movements gave away the presence of the units.

To enable units to communicate with each other we saw to it that each unit should know which units were in its immediate vicinity. They did not, however, know each other's hide-outs for security reasons, to avoid the danger of confessions extracted from members of groups who might fall into the hands of the enemy. Usually liaison and contact between units was maintained through a joint agent residing in a village who, as a rule, was ignorant of the exact location of the units' hide-outs. Thus each unit was able to inform its neighbours of what was happening inside its sector and, if severely pressed by the enemy, to withdraw from the area and take refuge in the neighbouring one where it could find shelter and food until the danger was over. For supplying the units we drew on the resources of the nearest towns. But in order to enable them to face the possibility of enemy searches lasting several days, before the beginning of the struggle stocks of food for fifteen to twenty men sufficient to last over a month were accumulated at monasteries and in mountain areas. Each unit had stocks of food and water to last as long as possible, often for a period exceeding one month. These food supplies, consisting of tinned foods, dried fruit and biscuits, together with water in barrels, were carefully preserved in underground hiding-places, securely closed and camouflaged inside the unit's zone and placed according to the unit's probable movements within the area. The enemy, in order to starve the groups out, carried out prolonged searches inside areas which were completely cut off by troops. The duration of these searches varied between fifteen and twenty days, and the longest of them in the Milikouri district lasted fifty-four days. Nevertheless, the enemy usually failed to achieve his object, because our forces, warned in time, either managed to slip away and break through the cordon, or, if they did not succeed in doing so, remained inside their hide-outs living on their stocks of provisions. Each guerrilla carried with him eight days' reserve rations in case of blockade. These rations proved to be very useful, even more so than the hidden stocks.

During my stay with the units I made the carrying of these reserve rations compulsory, not without some murmuring on the part of the men because of the extra weight. Later on, however, when experience had proved the wisdom of this precaution, every man was anxious to have reserve supplies fore more than eight days.

Liaison and supply agents. Great care must be taken in the selection of such agents and in regulating the functioning of their services, for the safety of units depends upon them.

The discovery of guerrilla hide-outs was due either to liaison and supply agents arrested by the enemy who gave away their location under interrogation or to the enemy's following on the tracks of such agents. Afxentiou's hiding-place was given away by his supply agent who was caught.

To reduce these risks I issued instructions that liaison and supply agents were not to come into immediate contact with the units nor were they to know their whereabouts. Both food supplies and correspondence were to be handed over to a trusted agent of each unit residing in a village, who was not to know the whereabouts of the unit. Each unit was to send one of its members to take delivery of the supplies and correspondence from the agent, under certain fixed conditions in each case. Thus, even if the supply agent or the intermediary was arrested, they would not know the unit's hide-out.

Great attention was also given to the guerrilla units' supplies of water. This can only come from springs or other running water, which makes it necessary for units to camp nearby. But this involved two serious risks.

First, in Cyprus springs are few and consequently it was easy for the enemy to keep them under observation and control.

Secondly, drawing of water from one spot leaves traces of footmarks which the enemy may notice both at the point where the water is drawn and along the adjacent paths. Some of our men were killed by soldiers lying in ambush near a stream where they used to go to fetch water.

During operations in mountain areas I often noticed footmarks which must have been made by soldiers wearing the special rubber-soled shoes with which they were issued for searches. This was so that they might not be heard, but they left their mark behind. In many cases, they left other traces in the form of fresh remains of food and empty cigarette packets.

Tasks, tactics and equipment of guerrilla units. The tasks given to guerrilla units were sudden attacks on the enemy's motorized forces, military installations and camps. The tactics to be employed as well as the necessary supplies of ammunition etc. were regulated according to the nature of the task. Our tactics consisted in dealing heavy blows from ambush and then slipping away rapidly under cover to escape from the net which the enemy would throw round the area and so avoid pursuit.

Ambushing of the enemy, our usual method of combat, proved the most effective one, and the enemy despite his superiority in means showed himself incapable of dealing with it.

There are two sorts of ambush, those planned beforehand and those organized on the spur of the moment against unexpected moving targets.

In the former instance careful preparation is necessary. Such attacks were nearly always successful, in spite of the precautions taken by the enemy. Usually these ambushes took place along the enemy's lines of communication and all necessary precautions had to be taken to avoid the ambush party's falling into a counter-ambush. In many cases the enemy was drawn to a particular spot by the sound of shots, and as a detachment hastened to investigate, it fell into the ambush prepared on the route.

In both cases the engagement must not last more than a few minutes. Success will depend on the selection of a suitable spot, on the strength of the attack and the effectiveness of the fire. The spot chosen must be one in which the enemy will be at a disadvantage from the point of view of returning fire and cover. When attacking a motorized column, a bend in the road should be chosen where the enemy is forced to reduce speed and the terrain on either side does not permit of the vehicles leaving the road nor of the enemy making use of his weapons. The site chosen must be such as to favour the assailant's fire and an easy and rapid withdrawal under cover. This last can be achieved either by a concealed route or, preferably, under cover of night, because night hampers the enemy's movements and in particular makes difficult intervention by the enemy air force. For this reason such operations best take place at sunset to take advantage of the few minutes of light for the attack or at any rate during the early evening hours, to allow sufficient time for the guerrillas to make their get-away. During the withdrawal roads and mountain paths should be avoided, because the enemy is sure to block them, in which case the retreating guerrillas may fall into an ambush. This danger is greater in an area where communications are good and plentiful, especially when the enemy has at his disposal rapid means of transport, helicopters in particular. During the two big operations undertaken by the British in the Spilia area in December 1955 and June 1956, I had to cover a great deal of ground under enemy pressure, especially during the June operations, yet I never followed the road but always chose very rough ground along the mountain sides. Whenever I had to cross a road I did so with the greatest precautions and only after careful reconnaissance. In this kind of operation the guerrilla must only carry a light load to be able to cover big distances. Our guerrilla bands often covered distances equal to two or more marches in a single night.

Armament. As a guerrilla band has to be small in numbers, its fire power must depend on a choice of the right weapons and a suitable combination of means of fire. Light automatic weapons and hand grenades are the best weapons for such occasions. It is also advisable that each unit have a bren gun for firing at medium distances. These weapons, however, are not enough and should be used with percussion or electrically detonated mines for sabotage on the roads to increase the number of casualties. One must remember that the guerrilla unit is always at a disadvantage from the point of view of equipment and fire power.

Mines should be used to blow up either the leading or rear vehicle of the enemy convoy – this to be determined by circumstances – to throw the convoy into disorder and compel the enemy to get down from the vehicles, thus exposing himself to the deadly fire of the attackers' automatics and hand grenades. This method of attack proved most effective and the enemy despite his superiority of means was unable to take successful counter-action. The only disadvantage in using mines was that they could not be employed on tarred roads, while on mud roads great care had to be taken to remove all traces of digging. On tarred roads we used what we called a 'small cannon', a tube of any size, closed at one end and filled with explosives or gunpowder mixed with fragments of iron which acted as projectiles. This contraption was made fast to a tree or wall by the side of the road at a suitable height and angle, so that when it was electrically detonated the projectile should strike the target. The 'small cannon', when used by our groups, yielded excellent results and very rarely failed to come off.

After our mines were perfected and more powerful, the results obtained were remarkable, vehicles being hurled a distance of as much as 16 to 22 yards, and hardly any of the occupants came off unharmed.

In the event of a guerrilla unit being surrounded by superior forces, the group should not attempt to fight its way out of the ring to escape unless there is no other way out. If surrounded, the group should hide to escape notice, then slip through gaps in the enemy lines and do a get-away. This requires a cool head on the part of the leader and all the members of the unit, and careful reconnaissance to discover the gaps which allow escape. On two occasions during the engagement near Spilia in December 1955 and Harding's big operation in July 1956, although I had been spotted and surrounded by infinitely superior forces and the enemy was confidently expecting to capture me any moment, I nevertheless succeeded in escaping in this way (see my *Memoirs*, pp. 17-78 and 101-108 of the Greek edition).

A British document[1] which fell into our hands laid down these instructions for coping with our activities:

'In every ambush, a part of the escort must try and remain outside the main fight and carry out a flanking movement on the terrorists' position. To do this, the maximum distance possible must be maintained between vehicles. When ambushed, the escort must dismount, investigate on foot and take the appropriate action having summed up the situation.

'Once in an ambush, the difficulty of driving through is clear. If this cannot be avoided, the officer/NCO IC should try to ensure that the vehicle does not stop until it is in dead ground from the terrorists' position and is able to take offensive action without being pinned down.

'There should be absolute alertness by all military personnel with weapons at instant readiness to fire. Flexibility of ambush drills to deal with any type of situation is essential.

'There is no standard type of terrorist ambush – they vary with the type of weapons and ammunition used.'

The above instructions at first sight seem quite correct and logical, nevertheless in practice they are often unrealistic.

Firstly, our ambushes did not conform to any fixed pattern. Sometimes a simple percussion mine detonated from a distance by a single individual was all there was to it, and so no flanking movement was possible. Secondly, there were four main factors taken into account in the preparation of an ambush, to secure success and escape, which always baffled the enemy: the element of surprise; the suitability of the terrain for attack; the possibility of an easy get-away; and good use of the means of fire. Finally, most important of all, the duration of an attack was very short, only four or five minutes, in which case

---

[1] Chief of Staff to H.E. the Governor's Secretariat, Nicosia, dated 3 December 1956.

the party or convoy attacked had no time to recover from their surprise and act. In every such ambush we took into account the number of vehicles and decided accordingly against which to direct our fire.

I stress once more that the men partaking in an ambush must be cool-headed and quick in order to take lightning decisions based on all the factors in a situation. Our men possessed these qualities and so hardly ever failed.

The main risk to which the attacker is exposed comes not from the ambushed party, which is always at a disadvantage *vis-à-vis* the ambusher, but from the possibility of the enemy's bringing up other forces quickly, blocking the attacker's probable route of escape and later surrounding the whole area so as to cut off his retreat. For this reason, the attacker's best chance of escape is to avoid being engaged for too long, to withdraw as rapidly as possible from the site of the ambush, taking cover all the time, and go to ground in a safe hiding-place.

For my instructions on the importance of ambushes and the tactics to be followed see Appendix, pp. 99-100.

SABOTAGE GROUPS. Sabotage was one of our most effective weapons and greatly harassed the enemy because, losses apart, it also affected the troops' morale.

Acts of sabotage, carried out systematically on a wide basis, made the enemy feel nowhere secure and became with him a sort of nightmarish obsession. In barracks and Army clubs, indeed wherever a British soldier could enter, we succeeded in having parties of saboteurs who also could make their way in and carry off a coup. The creation of these ubiquitous sabotage groups was a great achievement on the part of the Organization. Our targets were many: enemy forces on the move in motor vehicles, military bases (aircraft landing grounds, cantonments, etc.), Government buildings and police stations. Communications were not among our targets, because the enemy had a choice of so many that damage caused to any one would not have held him up in any way, whereas it would have caused serious hardship to the inhabitants.

Acts of sabotage were carried out by specially organized parties in towns and villages (these were composed either of persons wanted by the authorities and on the run or of ostensibly peace-loving citizens whom nobody knew or suspected); also by guerrilla units, by units of the Shotgun Commando Groups and special squads of Greek workmen employed inside military bases.

Specially worthy of mention are acts of sabotage committed inside the bases, because of the manner in which explosives and other incendiary material were introduced and the methodical and courageous way in which they were carried out. The inventiveness, boldness and organizing ability of those who undertook these missions made a great impression on everyone. They were daunted by no obstacle and every time would invent various ways of tricking the British. The latter were wholly unable to put an end to our activities in this field, and their bases, from beginning to end of the struggle, were constantly being rocked by explosions. Aircraft (in one case as many as five), landing grounds and buildings went up in flames. The moral effect of our successes was immense, quite apart from the enormous damage which amounted to several million pounds sterling.

In sabotage it was not possible to separate people into grades according to their speciality – all our men, to whatever category they belonged, had to be familiar with sabotage technique, seeing that sabotage entered into all our operations. Consequently, every one of our men was also a saboteur.

The materials they used were powerful explosive and incendiary mixtures, demolition primers, fulminate of mercury, electrical and ordinary detonators, clockwork mechanisms, incendiary bombs, percussion or electrically detonated mines. All these we managed to manufacture for ourselves with locally procured raw materials. This achievement on the part of our specialized squads was of great importance to the successful conduct of the struggle right to the end.

Parcel and letter traps are well known contrivances. Nevertheless, we used them successfully on a limited scale. The British Commissioner of Platrai was killed by a letter trap we sent to him. On its being opened, a special mechanism brought about an explosion. On another occasion a case was left inside a cave and the police were informed that it contained arms for EOKA. The NCO who tried to open the case was killed by the explosion.

EXECUTION GROUPS were composed of two or three men distinguished for courage, resourcefulness and marksmanship. They were set up in accordance with the basic principle of my General Plan that the enemy, wherever he happened to be, should never feel himself secure, and also to rid ourselves of certain dangerous individuals.

Our targets were any Englishman belonging to the armed forces, especially dangerous members of the Intelligence Service, interrogators who maltreated Greek detainees and Greek traitors in the service of the British. The weapons used were usually revolvers, sub-machine-guns and hand grenades.

Execution groups usually operated inside towns where the targets were easy. Their members were usually not persons wanted by the authorities but ordinary citizens moving about freely so as to be able to shadow their victim, prepare their plan of action and then attack him in the open street.

Everyone realizes how difficult their task was, demanding as it did courage, initiative, rapidity of thought, and physical strength. The execution of an individual in the middle of a street is no easy matter. First, the target must be shadowed in order to find out his habits – his route, the hours when he passes a particular spot, any precautionary measures he may happen to take, etc. After that, one must select the hour and place for the attack, and finally one must study one's own escape route. There are a host of other details to be remembered: how to avoid detection of the weapon on one's person in the event of search before carrying out the execution, and how to get rid of it after the act. An executioner should never carry his weapon himself, because the fact of its having been found on his person will be damning evidence against him. The weapon is better carried by some other person not liable to suspicion – a small boy, for instance, an old man or woman – and after the act a way should be found of passing the weapon to some third person who must hurry to get outside the cordon which is sure to be formed and take cover in a house agreed on beforehand. In such an operation one realizes how necessary it is to have the population on one's side.

Usually, each execution group had its auxiliary personnel, especially for the carrying of the lethal weapons. These auxiliaries were often young girls.

These missions were carried out with such skill that there was not a single case of an executioner being caught at work. Even when spotted they succeeded in getting away. Although many executions took place in the open street in the sight of dozens of persons, no Greek ever turned traitor. All preferred to undergo the hardship of the investigations, searches, fines and long days of house confinement which usually followed every execution.

In the *Chronicle of the Struggle*, which I intend to publish, several examples of executions are described. Our executions had intimidated the British authorities and had shaken their morale to such an extent that they were obliged to issue instructions like the following for the safety of British civilians: [1]

1. Never to accept a caller at their office, unless known to them personally or unless there were at least two members of their staff present.

2. Never to step out of their home or office without first making certain from a window that there was no one loitering near the door or by the garden entrance.

3. Never to open the door at night unless they recognized the voice of a friend.

4. To avoid regular habits such as leaving the house or office at the same time every day.

5. Not to trust their servants, Cypriots in particular, and to watch their movements.

6. To keep a dog if their home was isolated and without a telephone. Should they hear someone moving in the garden at night and receive no reply to their challenge, they should open the window, call out to him to go away and report the matter to the police.

7. To keep the window shutters closed.

8. To use a car and avoid going on foot.

9. To avoid visiting the Greek quarter of the town and to obtain supplies by telephone. Never to stand about in the street or, in case of absolute necessity, to stand with their backs to a wall.

10. To lock their car in the garage at night and not to leave it unattended and open during the day.

11. To avoid routes which might lead into traffic jams.

12. If they carried a pistol or revolver, to use a shoulder or belt holster, not to carry it in their pocket.

13. Not to drive too near to the pavement.

14. Should any suspicious person approach the vehicle when it slows down or halts, they should tell him to move on. Should he attempt to argue or refuse, they should grab him to see if he is armed.

15. Should an individual approach the car holding a pistol or attempt to draw one, they should not hesitate to shoot him.

16. Attention was also drawn to the possibility of a bomb being placed in an office drawer to explode when the drawer was opened. People should limit the number of drawers used and keep the keys on their person.

[1] *Translator's note:* Summary of instructions issued by Divisionary Police Headquarters, Nicosia, dated 1 December 1957.

Besides the precautionary measures taken for the protection of British subjects, the authorities also took the following steps: special groups of soldiers were placed on the roofs of houses in the most dangerous areas to keep a watch on the street, in positions from which they could easily fire at any suspicious person below. Frequent patrols used to go along the streets and search all civilians whoever they might be.

In view of these measures one can realize the great difficulties encountered by our groups in carrying out their missions. Of course, our use of execution groups came in for criticism on the part of our opponents who called us 'murderers' because we struck from behind. Such a charge is, to say the least, naïve, because to kill your opponent by assailing him at his weakest point, from the side or rear, is a tactic as old as Alexander the Great, Epaminondas and Marathon, and in more modern times was adopted during the wars of Frederick the Great and Napoleon. What would the critics say if a general were to make a frontal attack against a much stronger opponent, thereby leading his soldiers to a useless death? They would of course demand that he be court-martialled or at least cashiered. What would they say, on the other hand, if another general, by a skilful manoeuvre brought his troops to the opponent's rear and directed his men's fire at the enemy's back? Far from calling him a murderer, they would applaud him. The tactics of our execution groups, who attacked the weak side of their target, form a parallel, on a smaller scale, to this last example.

A serious problem we had to face in regulating the activities of our saboteurs, execution and other groups in the towns was the curfew. But this difficulty was also surmounted. Once more it was proved that 'where there is a will there is a way'. Single men or small groups of two or three men, who take up their position near their target, with courage can always find an opportunity of slipping through and carrying out their mission. The attack on the English College in Nicosia on 20 June 1958, carried out by a group of eleven men, took place during a curfew, and the same applies to several other important operations, especially executions. Occasionally, if there was a curfew on, arrangements were made for small groups from villages adjoining the area under curfew to slip through and attack isolated targets. This was done mainly for psychological reasons – in order to prove that even during a curfew our fighters were ready to operate and were not afraid.

Whenever the British imposed curfews lasting many days, in order not to paralyse work and the movements of the population, they confined the curfew to persons below the age of 27 in the belief that the hard core of our members were young men and youths below that age. We bore this in mind and consequently our special squads of curfew-breakers were composed of persons above the age of 27. The British, who failed to notice this, continued to maintain this age distinction.

SHOTGUN COMMANDO GROUPS (OKT) were created as part of the General Plan which provided for turning the whole island into a field of battle. For want of more suitable weapons we armed them with shotguns we had taken from the owners. Besides these, the groups all carried hand grenades, mines and occasionally a light automatic. The shotguns came in extremely useful in ambushes. For their greater effectiveness we manufactured special shot of a bigger calibre than usual so as to increase their range and deadliness. OKT members were usually persons wanted by the authorities, but among them there were also a few against whom there was no charge, who went about their daily business as if they were ordinary peace-loving citizens. The strength of OKT groups was kept to 5-6 men for the same reasons which held good for the guerrilla units.

The OKT members had hide-outs, usually in villages. These were different from the type of mountain guerrilla hide-out – being inside houses they were more comfortable and the entrance and construction were adapted to the conformation of the building so as not to present a suspicious or abnormal appearance. The entrance was usually camouflaged in the door of a cupboard or concealed by a movable book-case, and the shelter itself was excavated under the floor.

The mission of OKT groups was to lay ambushes. Generally, they can be described as guerrilla units for operating in open country down in the plains, under quite different conditions from those prevailing in hilly country. They usually operated at night which offered better opportunities for assailing a target and when it was much easier to get away after the accomplishment of their mission and go underground.

Each sector was free to create as many OKT units as it wished, provided the number did not exceed the area's 'saturation point'.

Like the guerrilla bands, OKT units varied their tactics and did not stick to any particular formula. These tactics were either dictated by the central organization or depended on the local conditions and were carried out on the initiative of the sector leaders or even of the group itself. The OKT groups gradually became so experienced that I left full initiative to the sectors as to how they were to operate, only intervening in exceptional cases. They carried out their mission exemplarily and became the bogey of the British who could no longer circulate freely in the open country. Their conduct, when discovered and forced to give battle, was truly heroic. Worthy of special mention are the engagement near Lysa of 23 August 1958 and the battle of Liopetri of 2 September 1958.[1]

[1] See my *Memoirs*, pp. 296-7 of the Greek edition.

PART III

5. Conclusions from the Cyprus Liberation Campaign

The conclusions to be drawn from the previous pages are either of a general nature, holding good in the case of all similar campaigns, or else are applicable only to the special circumstances of the campaign in Cyprus. For, as I have previously emphasized, each case demands its own special strategy and tactics and presents its own particular problems.

STRATEGY

1. A leader planning a guerrilla war should first make a general investigation and careful study of the special conditions, after which he should draw up in all secrecy a suitable plan and prepare the ground for the struggle. Throughout this initial period the element of surprise should constitute the central axis round which all his arrangements should turn. Surprise is all-important to success.

2. The objective of the struggle should be clearly and realistically defined. This is a basic requirement. For whereas in conventional warfare one's aim should always be to crush the enemy's forces, the aim of guerrilla warfare, whether as a self-contained action in a liberation struggle or resistance movement, or else in combination with a war of conventional type as part of a general plan, must vary according to the nature of the campaign, depending on whether it is an independent operation or forms part of a general strategic plan in a conventional war.

3. In the Cyprus liberation campaign, where the strategic objective was to harass and wear down the opponent through a long-duration effort, our strategy consisted in turning the whole island into a single field of battle in which there was no distinction between front and rear, so that the enemy should at no time and in no place feel himself secure. The enemy never knew where and when we might strike. This strategy achieved the dispersal, intimidation and wearing down of the enemy's forces and especially serious consequences resulting from our use of surprise.

4. There exists a great disparity between the resources of which the leader of a guerrilla movement can dispose and those of his opponent.

So the former should never allow himself to be drawn into pitched battles. Otherwise he loses all the advantages of guerrilla warfare and has to apply the strategy and methods of conventional warfare where he is bound to find himself at a disadvantage and naturally to face defeat. Throughout the four years' duration of the struggle in Cyprus, although repeatedly challenged by the opponent, I avoided all exhibitions of strength and stuck from beginning to end to the form of guerrilla warfare as originally conceived by me, for which I was organized, and which alone was within my capabilities. Harding himself is said to have confided to his immediate entourage: 'I did not succeed in luring Grivas.' In Greece we have a characteristic example of the failure to observe the above principle on the part of the leadership of the Communist rebellion of 1947-9. The rebellion, as we all know, originally started with guerrilla bands operating over the whole of Greece from Cape Tainaron to Macedonia and Thrace. By waging successful guerrilla warfare, these bands were able seriously to threaten the country's lawful régime, until the various bourgeois political parties, in the face of the common danger, found themselves forced to come to an agreement and form a coalition government. Nevertheless, the Communist rebellion continually gained ground and guerrilla bands even used to descend from their bases in the mountains of the Peloponnese, Thessaly, Macedonia and Epirus, and attack towns, railway-stations and other centres. The situation had become critical. The Communists, intoxicated by their successes and without correctly gauging their own capabilities, attempted to convert their guerrilla struggle into a conventional war, mainly for political reasons. But they were not yet in any position to bring such a war to a victorious conclusion. Obsessed by the idea that they ought to have under their complete control a fixed strip of territory where they could set up a Government of 'Free Greece', they chose an area in the Pindus mountains where they established a defensive line. There, however, their forces sustained a crushing defeat at the hands of the infinitely stronger National Army, and the remnants of their forces had to take refuge in the neighbouring Communist countries.

A similar mistake was made by the leaders of the recent uprising in Oman. The rebels, being much weaker than the British, concentrated their forces inside some old forts where they prepared to put up a resistance, instead of resorting to guerrilla tactics in open country and harassing the British. Thus, of their own free will, they shut themselves up in confined positions where they offered themselves as targets. The result was that they were crushed by the British air force and artillery.

In Algeria, the O A S leaders confined themselves to street fighting and sabotage, mainly in the cities of Algiers and Oran. They thereby exposed their own forces as targets to the far superior forces of the French Government. Having failed to win over the army in Algeria or to carry on a guerrilla campaign in open country in combination with underground activity inside the towns, they were doomed and failed to attain their purpose. It would perhaps have been better had they concentrated their efforts on metropolitan France and sought to overthrow General de Gaulle, after which, once in power, they could have settled the Algerian question as they thought best.

5. Superiority in numbers does not count in guerrilla warfare, provided guerrilla tactics are used. Then the advantage does not lie in numbers but in adopting suitable strategy and tactics. One can realize how true this is when one thinks that during E O K A's struggle a mere handful of combatants, who never had more than 100 automatic weapons and 500-600 shotguns, besides a quantity of explosives for sabotage, succeeded in putting up a successful fight, in a small island, for four years, against a highly organized army of 40,000 men backed by a mighty empire.

In guerrilla warfare there are times when the terrain, whatever its nature, must be regarded as having reached 'saturation point'. This, contrary to the case in conventional warfare, is more likely to happen in flat than in mountainous country.

6. There are no such things as fixed 'types' of guerrilla warfare to which one must adhere, and there is no pre-determined strategy. There are as many different kinds of strategy as there are kinds of guerrilla warfare.

7. It is neither logical nor practical to try to counter guerrilla warfare with strategy based solely on force. Statesmanship and diplomacy are needed to isolate the guerrillas from the population. The leadership of the forces fighting the guerrillas needs special methods of combat and a proper organization, as dictated by circumstances, to track down, displace and force them from their hiding-places and thus obtain the chance to deal them a decisive blow. You cannot chase monkeys with elephants. Cunning can only be met by greater cunning and mobility by greater mobility. Strength alone soon evaporates and may even prove dangerous to those who use it.

8. Morale plays an all-important role. It needs great moral fibre on the part of both people and fighters to enable them to endure hard-

ships, privations and dangers. No effort is too great to secure morale. The youth will always be the foundation and nursery of every liberation struggle and the leader should always turn in that direction.

9. The choice of the leader is a decisive factor. Daring, resourcefulness, a cool head, dash, but also prudence, cunning, persistence in the struggle – all these are qualities which he must possess. Above all, however, he must have the gift of inspiring confidence in the people and his men by his own actions.

In Cyprus, in the special conditions which governed the organization and conduct of the struggle, a leading role was played by the ability and courage of the local commanders, suitably guided from above, and by our use of the most appropriate methods of combat. The nature of the terrain was a secondary factor. One would have expected our activities to be on a much bigger scale in the mountain areas and much more limited in the plains and non-wooded districts. Yet I at once realized that this was not strictly true and that it was perfectly possible to carry out important operations in the lowlands as well. That is why I modified my original General Plan and decided to transform the whole island into one general field of combat. It was for this purpose that I created the O K T (Shotgun Commando Groups).

The truth of the above is confirmed by the events themselves. Thus in the Famagusta sector (Mesaoria plain) the terrain is entirely flat and nearly treeless. Nevertheless, the activity shown by this sector was most extensive, so much so that the British called the area 'The Death Zone'. The Karpassia sector also consists of a narrow strip of land which can easily be blockaded by land and sea and thoroughly combed, because there are only low hills, especially towards the north. Yet this sector too showed a great deal of activity. The same can be said about the Dheftera-Orini sector. On the other hand, the Morphou and Akaki sectors yielded poor results.

In the mountain sectors, which were the main scene of guerrilla activity, we found that wherever able and courageous leadership was lacking, the results were rather disappointing, whereas, as soon as an area came under capable leadership, its achievements were satisfactory and often striking.

For me, at any rate, it remains axiomatic that in guerrilla warfare, with able and courageous leadership, one can take on any undertaking, whatever the nature of the terrain.

TACTICS

1. As in strategy, so in the tactics of guerrilla warfare, there only exist special cases, each one of which has its appropriate method of fighting. In the Cypriot liberation campaign we used the weapons and other means already mentioned. We gave our preference to none, but co-ordinated and combined them according to the needs of the moment. It follows that all means are good and one must be prepared to employ all of them on an extensive scale.

2. Sabotage, well-organized and on a big scale, yields very good results and, besides the casualties it inflicts, also reacts on the enemy's morale as he nowhere feels secure.

3. Whatever the means employed, the organization should be based on small units the size of which should depend not only on the needs of any particular operation but also on the necessity of making an easy get-away and remaining concealed, and equally, during periods of inaction, on being able to obtain supplies while in hiding, without attracting the attention of the enemy. Where it is necessary to employ a larger force for a particular operation, additional men can be obtained by the participation of several units, which after the action return to their respective areas.

4. Distribution of the various units and resources over the territory as well as the display of action must be such as to give the enemy an impression of ubiquitous activity and constant readiness to attack, but at the same time to avoid detection care should be taken to refrain from unnecessary action.

5. The tactics should consist in sudden blows, of short duration, boldly executed, followed by instant and rapid withdrawal. The targets chosen should be at a distance from the hiding-places of the units so as to avoid encirclement of the area and the danger of discovery.

6. I wish to stress the importance of the helicopter in guerrilla war-fare. In my opinion this weapon will play a very effective part in any future operations of this kind. We in Cyprus, of course, could not use them. The British employed helicopters but on a limited scale and not always in the proper manner, mostly for carrying out reconnais-sance against guerrilla bands in the mountains and over inhabited areas where operations were proceeding. A Bulletin issued by the British forces in Cyprus on 1 July 1957 laid down that helicopters should be used to blockade villages or areas being searched for wanted

persons, in combination with the ground forces. A helicopter would land in the village to announce the imposition of a curfew while a number of others would fly low over the village. No other important use of helicopters came to our notice save for limited transports of small forces during operations in the mountains. These did not trouble us much. On many occasions when we found ourselves in a tight corner under pressure from the British, we came to realize how serious things would have been if proper use had been made of the helicopter, and how different the position would have been had we had helicopters at our disposal. The helicopter can land on the roughest wooded and mountainous ground, provided it can find a few square yards to alight on. Usually a level bit of ground measuring about forty square yards, with free access at the sides, will suffice. Because of its relatively slow speed and its ability to fly very low, almost touching the ground, the helicopter is an ideal means of transport for small forces, as the men can descend by a ladder while the helicopter is in flight, without the machine needing to touch down. A helicopter can also pick up men from the ground by the same means and take on supplies by lowering a winch.

The helicopter's only disadvantage is its vulnerability because of its low speed and its proximity to the ground. This however is partly counterbalanced by the fact that in guerrilla warfare the opponent does not have sufficient and suitable fire power. Moreover the helicopter is able to escape notice because of its ability to fly along deep and concealed folds in the ground, so that enemy fire is less effective. The above peculiarities determine the missions that can be assigned to the helicopter in guerrilla warfare.

The principal of these missions are:

1. For the attacking party: dropping small specially trained units in the defenders' rear so as to occupy their route of retreat or to sabotage communications; rapid transport of forces to inaccessible points in the area of operations; discovery of enemy hide-outs and movements, especially in wooded country; to direct the movements of ground troops when searching suspicious points.

2. For the defending party: rapid transport of forces to spots which, if occupied by the enemy, would present a threat of encirclement or would cut off the defenders' line of retreat; dropping units in the attacker's rear in order to cut off or threaten his communications or directly to menace sections engaged in attack.

3. For both attacker and defender: carrying out reconnaissance during operations; intervention on the ground by firing on the opposing forces; liaison between Command and sections; urgent conveyance of supplies or transport of wounded.

6. *General Conclusions on Guerrilla Warfare*

THE STRATEGIC OBJECTIVE

If we consider the two main forms of guerrilla warfare, namely independent military action or as part of a general strategic plan, it is clear that, in the first case, the guerrilla movement is the sole instrument of the political aim pursued, whereas in the second case it is merely an auxiliary instrument towards attaining the aim of the war, the main part being played by the regular army.

In the first case, one has to ask oneself: can such a struggle, employing guerrilla methods alone, bring about the solution by its own means – i.e. destroy the enemy forces or wear them down to the point where they will be forced to negotiate for peace? (This, of course, is the strategic objective of conventional warfare.)

Many believe that guerrilla warfare cannot achieve a solution unless the guerrilla forces are finally constituted into a regular army, which can take the field and meet the enemy face to face. In this case, guerrilla warfare is merely the start – an early phase of wider military operations which must follow in order to produce a final result. Those who belong to this school of thought quote the examples of Mao Tse Tung in China and Fidel Castro in Cuba (see Che Guevara on *Guerrilla Warfare*). But in order to draw correct conclusions we should extend our investigation. For in each case there are two principal factors which exercise a decisive influence – the objective and the means employed. In the cases of China and Cuba, the objective was a Communist Social Revolution. As regards means, Mao had at his disposal unlimited resources and a vast territory. Castro too had at his disposal, though on nothing like the same scale, very considerable resources and territory. On the other hand, the resistance movements of the Second World War as well as the liberation movements of Cyprus and Algeria, both of which used guerrilla methods, had essentially different aims and means.

I suggest that the above-mentioned belief is not wholly correct. The

77

best proof is provided by the Cypriot liberation campaign which from start to finish used guerrilla methods in the rural districts and underground warfare in the towns, and where a mere handful of combatants for four full years was able to stand up successfully to a regular army which towards the end numbered 40,000 men; which moreover compelled the political leadership to reach a settlement of the Cyprus question even if, as things turned out, this settlement did not satisfy the Cypriot demand for self-determination.

I hold that it is sometimes possible for a guerrilla organization, as an independent military movement, to attain the desired political objective alone. The strategic aim must be continuously to wear down the opposing forces till it is impossible for them to put down the movement. Thereby there eventually arise internal political difficulties in the enemy's country and external complications in the international field, leading to a demand for a political solution. Consequently, this kind of warfare must be mainly one of attrition and endurance and, as such, demands the methods of combat best adapted to the circumstances.

Such were both the Cypriot and Algerian liberation struggles. For seven whole years the Algerian forces succeeded in holding their own against the greatly superior forces of a well organized French army, numbering some 450,000 men, and prevented them winning a decisive victory. Finally, in order to avoid further bloodshed, the French were compelled to agree to a solution which satisfied the Algerian people's demand for self-determination. During the hostilities there were neither victors nor conquered, only continuous casualties and attrition which finally obliged the French to give way to the Algerians' persistent demand. Will-power and fighting spirit enabled the Algerians to prevail and obtain the historic recognition of their claims, guided by a political leadership which never wavered and was inspired by faith in the justice of their cause.

In the second case, where guerrilla warfare is subordinate to a general strategic plan, the strategy of a guerrilla struggle is merely accessory to the main objective – the complete defeat of the enemy forces. Such a plan can take the following forms:

1. Offensive Strategic Plan. Guerrilla warfare inside enemy territory achieving interruption of communications, sabotage of war industries, disturbances in the rear of their army, etc., thereby diverting enemy forces and affecting the people's morale, and lastly the organization of insurrections, provided the circumstances are favourable and there exist friendly elements among the population. The basic objective is to impair the enemy's capacity for war, by attacking targets the destruction of which will promote the execution of the general strategic plan. These operations may take the form either of commando raids against a particular target or of general guerrilla activity in part or parts of the enemy's territory. This guerrilla activity will be undertaken either by friendly elements within enemy territory, secretly organized in time of peace, or by specially trained commandos dropped by parachute during hostilities, or by both.

2. Defensive Strategic Plan. Guerrilla warfare within one's own territory in areas which have fallen into enemy hands as the result of evacuation or the inability to hold them. This will mean organizing a guerrilla war in abandoned sections of national territory, on the basis of the original plan, with the possibility of extending it to the whole territory in the event of this being abandoned either as the result of the allied forces' defeat or as part of an operation arising from a general plan involving a coalition of states.

A struggle of this kind took place during the Second World War in Axis-occupied countries, where resistance movements were organized. These movements, however, were spontaneous and had not been planned beforehand, with the result that they were not uniformly successful and were exploited by international Communism, as happened in Greece, Yugoslavia and elsewhere. Nowadays such a struggle should be planned in peacetime, in absolute secrecy, as part of a general strategic plan. Only thus will it have better chances of success, and not run the risk of being exploited by any party. Thus the means will be forthcoming and there will be plenty of time to organize the struggle, the success of which is dependent on a combination of local factors.

Supplies and equipment of guerrilla forces can be secured both by using local resources and also through foreign aid by supplies being dropped from the air or otherwise, as happened during the Second World War when the Greek guerrilla forces were supplied with arms in this way.

FORMS AND DEVELOPMENTS

Because of its peculiar character the Cypriot liberation campaign, like any similar one, cannot serve as a blue-print for this type of struggle. But its study can serve merely to supplement a knowledge of guerrilla warfare and also to illustrate a line of thought and action which may help one to solve the innumerable problems which may present themselves in each special case.

The Cypriot liberation campaign, as an independent armed movement, used methods which in the future may be employed in similar struggles in the event of a conflict in countries occupied by the enemy or within enemy territory. The struggle, as a subsidiary part of a conventional war, will start with the organization of small guerrilla and saboteur groups. Its aim, initially at any rate, will not be total defeat of the enemy forces but to occupy them and wear them down, as stated by the General Plan. Eventually there will come the final blow to be struck at the opposing army, when the guerrilla forces must be ready to intervene at the proper moment. All the guerrilla movements to which we have referred started with quite small guerrilla groups.

Mao Tse Tung's original force consisted of workmen, but after its collapse he repeated his effort by recruiting peasants in rural areas and with his promises of agrarian reform he succeeded in forming quite powerful guerrilla bands. By employing these bands in guerrilla tactics, he was able to deal his opponents severe blows. Gradually he united the bands and succeeded in forming an army which after the withdrawal of the Japanese was able to stand up to Chiang Kai-shek's army which he finally expelled from China.

Fidel Castro, on the other hand, landed in Cuba at the head of some small guerrilla units whose numbers gradually swelled until he was able to form a revolutionary army (see Che Guevara on *Guerrilla Warfare*).

In both these cases there was a predetermined plan which aimed at gaining control over China and Cuba respectively. The basic principle, in both cases, was to swell the strength of the guerrilla movement not only by increasing the number of bands but also by amalgamating these into a regular army that would be in a position to fight it out with the opposing army. The main objective was the complete defeat of the opponent. This was well within the bounds of possibility and was the proper course to adopt. For all the necessary resources of manpower and material were available, and there was the added advantage of a vast expanse of territory which made it easy to form an army. This was the only way in which the objective – namely, the defeat of the opposing forces – could be achieved.

Mustafa Kemal's movement in Asia Minor was of the same character. He too started off by organizing bands of irregulars – called *chetés* – taking advantage of the vast expanse of Anatolia which served as his base. The bands found a safe place from which to operate, and also had on their side the population from which he could recruit men and draw supplies. Moreover he received large quantities of war material from our former allies the French and Italians as well as from Soviet Russia. Thus, little by little, he was enabled to form a regular army which in the end was able to stand up to the Greek forces.

In all three cases there existed all the necessary factors for the transformation of the guerrilla bands into a regular army.

PREPARATION AND CONDUCT OF OPERATIONS

The organization of a guerrilla war must necessarily pass through two stages – the stage of preparation and the operational stage.

Preparation. Secrecy is the basic requirement, because it makes surprise of the enemy possible, but secrecy can only be achieved by limiting numbers. So one must initially choose only a small number of companions on whose discretion one may rely. Each member should only be acquainted with what concerns him directly. In working out the programme every care must be taken to prevent leakages. An espionage and counter-espionage service should be organized to keep in touch with the enemy's information service and also to keep under observation the members of the organization, their contacts and their methods of work.

Conduct of operations. Should the forces employed in the struggle allow more extensive activity than we could undertake in Cyprus and if the area of operations is larger, then both the manner in which the force will be deployed and the strategy and tactics to be adopted will differ considerably.

One would start by organizing groups of guerrillas and saboteurs, at first in accessible mountain areas where they could be trained in safety. It is also advisable to organize a small number of such units within the enemy's own territory. Sabotage squads could operate inside the area occupied by the enemy, especially in towns.

As the forces increase, a secure base should be organized somewhere difficult of approach, if possible, inaccessible. It should be sufficiently extensive to avoid complete encirclement in an attack by the enemy and at the same time allow the guerrilla bands to move about with ease and in safety, without it being possible for the enemy to ascertain its exact location. The security system should aim mainly at giving timely warning of enemy movements, through observers and mobile patrols within the area of the base as well as through agents posted inside the enemy zone. It is also desirable that the base should, as far as possible, have its own sources of supplies as well as offer a possibility of landing supplies by air or sea. Access to the sea is all-important, provided one's own side holds the supremacy at sea. The base will also serve as a starting-point from which an attack can be launched against the enemy's positions – communications, towns and other important centres.

The enemy should never be allowed a moment's rest. The guerrilla groups should always be on the offensive, for constant activity is the best way of maintaining morale and keeping the struggle alive. These operations, to yield full results, must be combined with acts of sabotage by the units within the enemy zone.

As soon as the position has been stabilized, provided always that the forces engaged in the struggle are adequate, the base can be enlarged and even extended into enemy territory. But this will create various problems not only of combat but more especially of supply, security of communications, liaison, etc.

The system of civil administration to be established in the occupied area should be studied beforehand to permit of services being set up and functioning immediately. During the Cyprus campaign such a question did not arise and consequently no such measures had to be taken.

The enemy too, one must remember, will have organized his own underground resistance in these areas. It is therefore essential to dislocate his underground organization, win over the population by administrative measures and secure new sources of supply.

Generally speaking, throughout the period during which guerrilla methods will be employed, both strategy and tactics should conform to the pattern of a constant offensive maintained by raids into enemy territory, followed by withdrawal to the base. The enemy must be continually harassed. Guerrilla forces are like a fly which keeps on teasing, flying away when brushed off only to return again to the attack. In the event of the enemy staging a major offensive, one should not present to him a firm front or fixed targets. He will then be hitting air. Guerrilla forces should deploy to effect their escape, they may even sometimes have to break up for a time, to come together again as soon as the danger is past. A static defence would be madness.

Only if the forces available are sufficient and the objective demands it, should an attempt be made to inflict on the enemy a final blow. This will demand the organization of a revolutionary army, with its own peculiar composition and organization. It will need a plan which will among other things provide for the intervention of friendly elements – guerrillas and saboteurs – inside enemy territory. Such assistance can be extremely valuable not only in the capture of towns and other points, but also in the harassing and destruction of enemy communications, in creating confusion in his rear and in disorganizing his front.

Guerrilla warfare, as a phase of a campaign, will in the future assume a more concrete form and will be extensively employed in the preliminary stages of a conflict or during the main operations.

Besides the cases mentioned in Chapter 2, 'What are the Prospects for Guerrilla Warfare?', two special cases should at this point be mentioned:

1. A defeated army, which is not in a position to carry on a war, should be able to start guerrilla activities by breaking up into small groups so as to continue the struggle under another form. In such circumstances what is needed is a leader and a determined plan. This can either be improvised or may already have been foreseen. Things would have turned out very differently in Greece during the Second World War if the army in Albania after its victory over the Italians had broken up into small units, instead of capitulating to the Germans, and carried on the struggle in the mountains of Epirus, Thessaly and Macedonia. Thus the guerrilla war which started later on, under largely Communist leadership, would have been conducted by the national army under nationalist military leadership. Such a decision had in fact been taken by the Second Infantry Division, of which I was Chief of Staff; parleys had already taken place with the Division's subordinate commands, and movements had already begun with a view to transferring the Division to the Pindus range. Unfortunately, the Division's intentions and movements came to the notice of the higher command and not only was the attempt frustrated but also the Second Division was actually the first to be disarmed by the Germans outside Yannina.

2. Every army, as soon as it occupies hostile territory, should have ready an organization of special units to be used to put down any attempt on the part of the defeated enemy to start guerrilla activity within the territory. An army's offensive plan should always provide for such a contingency.

WESTERN POLICY TOWARDS GUERRILLA MOVEMENTS
IN FRIENDLY COUNTRIES

The Communist bloc today has launched guerrilla wars in countries which are under the control of the West or are friendly to it. These guerrilla activities have helped to promote Soviet policy and are undoubtedly a preliminary phase in the Soviet General Strategic Plan for an offensive to which they are auxiliary. These local wars are continually spreading in Asia, Africa and Latin America. By them Russian policy seeks to weaken the position of the West and improve its own strategic bases, working towards a subsequent trial of strength but without immediately risking war.

Until now the Western powers have not put up any serious opposition to this policy of expansion, with the result that important strategic bastions are falling under Communist control. The reasons for this are the following:

Firstly, the policy of the Western powers in countries exposed to Communist attack aims mainly at protecting the lives and economic interests of their own citizens rather than at defending the more general interests of mankind and of their own countries. The military forces carrying out this policy are not regarded, according to the prevailing view, as constituting armed intervention or a declaration of war. Help is confined to giving occasional counsel and material aid to the countries attacked, as happened at the time of the Communist intervention in Greece in 1946-9. Western policy avoids complete involvement in the defence of these countries against the danger that threatens them. The result of this Western policy is that the Communist peril is constantly spreading and getting nearer to their own countries. When Communism finally reaches them they will regret it bitterly but then it may be too late. In South Vietnam, for instance, Communist infiltration today has reached serious proportions, yet the United States confines itself to the sending of equipment and a few officers in a purely advisory role.

Secondly, the United Nations are unable to take effective action in such cases because of disagreement among members and the systematic veto exercised by the Soviet Union.

Thirdly, the Western powers do not possess the necessary experience of guerrilla warfare or suitable expeditionary forces organized for the conduct of guerrilla operations.

Can one believe that, with expeditionary corps of the kind represented by the Marines of the 6th American Fleet in the Mediterranean, movements like the ones I have mentioned can be put down? I fear that the initiative has already passed to the Communist bloc, which, ignoring all conventions, has already acquired the necessary experience for the conduct of guerrilla warfare or interventionary action.[1]

The policy at present pursued by the Communist bloc is very different from that of the West. The Communist bloc is in a position to start a war and keep it within local dimensions, whereas the strategy of the West only envisages total war but does not provide for decisive intervention in the case of a limited local war, however great the interests endangered. Consequently the West remains a mere spectator of Communist infiltration in all the continents.

I personally think that a more realistic policy is required on the part of the Western powers. The aims of this policy should be three:

1. Active opposition to the spread of Communist infiltration. Let them not deceive themselves. This growing infiltration is merely the preliminary stage of a general conflict. It aims at securing for the Communist bloc offensive bases to serve later as the starting-point for the enslavement of mankind.

2. A counter-offensive to free the countries now under Communist control from Communist domination, by helping them to organize resistance movements, as the Soviet Union does when it stirs up revolution in those parts of the globe which serve her policy. To achieve this end, the West must, first, form properly trained forces to assist in the organization or suppression of guerrilla wars in other countries; second, create an organization to learn Communist intentions in good time and to keep an eye on preparations for intervention in countries which are not at present under Communist control; third, a more realistic policy to remove the causes which provoke revolutions and

---

[1] At Fort Galing in the Panama Canal Zone, there functions the so-called 'American Military School of the Caribbean', with U.S. administration, where officers from nearly all the Latin American countries are taught how to deal with sabotage and guerrilla action and learn the strategy of 'band warfare'.

This school, which has been in existence for thirteen years, gives both theoretical and practical lessons in jungle warfare.

But any military school must create a tradition and lay down rules and methods—above all, both teaching staff and pupils must believe in what they teach or are taught and must attach due importance to this. Is this the case at this school? I very much doubt it, judging by the small importance so far attached to this subject and by the manner in which the United States has hitherto dealt with this aspect of war.

thereby deprive the Communist bloc of its most important weapon – the slogans of political and social injustice which Communism exploits in the most effective way to stir up peoples against their existing régimes.

3. The strategic plans of the Western powers in anticipation of a general conflict should be revised to provide for this new form of warfare, if this has not been done already.

We do not know exactly how the Western Alliance plans to deal with Russian infiltration and the whole question of guerrilla warfare in a future conflict. From information that has reached the Press it would appear that the Pentagon originally had objections to U.S. forces being used in any kind of war other than a conventional war but finally consented to the formation of a special military force to conduct guerrilla warfare. The first U.S. units of this force, according to the same source, began arriving in Vietnam in January 1962 and are taking part in the operations as 'military advisers' to the Vietnamese Government forces.

The use of this force in this particular way is an indication of how it is constituted and of what are its capacities of action. It makes one doubt whether this force is in a position to serve as shock troops in the event of a guerrilla war; still more, whether in the event of a general conflict it will be able to undertake, either inside the United States or in foreign theatres of war, the kind of operations I described in Part I (pp. 1-3). It is possible however that this force is merely a start – an experiment towards the final organization and future development of such forces.

Let us hope so, in case we are again taken by surprise, as we were in both World Wars by German strategy.

THE PROBABLE EFFECT ON STRATEGY AND TACTICS OF NUCLEAR WEAPONS

It would be dangerous to be dogmatic about the extent to which strategy and tactics are likely to be influenced by the use of nuclear weapons and the conquest of space. The work is still in the experimental stage and there is every possibility of an antidote as well as a means of protection being discovered.

Whatever the developments may be, it may be taken as certain that the use of nuclear weapons will require the dispersal of the ground forces both of defender and attacker as one means of protection against the new weapons. Faced with the terrific destructive power of these new engines of war, we must seek to protect our forces by dispersal. This will demand new methods of combat.

In defence, continuous and dense occupation of a territory to a relatively small depth, and, in attack, the close offensive formation will both certainly undergo substantial changes. This is not the moment to express an opinion on the strategy and tactics of the future. We merely refer to the question in order to emphasize that the methods of guerrilla warfare will play an important part in any future conflict, because of the dispersal of forces which is a characteristic of this type of warfare.

The range of nuclear weapons and their terrifying results, plus the possibility of an enemy launching a guerrilla war inside a country will convert that country into a single field of battle. There will be no front and no rear and virtually the whole of the population will become combatants.

The only difference will be as regards the means and methods which will be adopted in each particular territory. Consequently it is incumbent on political leaders to show greater interest and take a more active part in the preparation of the strategic plans of their respective countries, instead of placing their entire trust in the services and blindly following their advice. This means that the political leaders should be fully cognizant of and in close touch with the strategic policy of their country which should be carefully reshaped.

THE ROLE OF THE NAVY

Finally, there is one question which is of particular interest to us in Greece, and that is the role of the Navy in a guerrilla war. The Navy is of special importance to Greeks because of the oceanography of our seas, the many scattered islands and our highly indented coast-line.

A special kind of Navy is needed for a guerrilla war. We can learn much from our War of Independence in 1821. The study of our glorious past and of the Navy's contribution to that struggle will help us in our conclusions about the role of the Navy in the case under consideration.

Appendix

APPENDIX

I

Preliminary General Plan of Insurrectionary Action in Cyprus

(This plan was drawn up in Greece and served as a basis for the further organization and conduct of the struggle.)

AIM

By deeds of heroism and self-scarifice to draw the attention of international public opinion, especially among the allies of Greece, to the Cyprus question which might prove a source of trouble to them unless a settlement were found that satisfied our claims.

By continuously harassing the British in Cyprus, we must show that we are firmly determined not to yield, whatever the sacrifice, but that on the contrary we are prepared to continue until our aim is attained.

The struggle will be carried on until international diplomacy exercised through the United Nations, and the British in particular, is compelled to examine the Cyprus problem and reach a speedy settlement in accordance with the aspirations of the Cypriot people and the whole Greek nation.

PROCEDURE

Activity will mainly lie in attacks on the British Government forces in Cyprus, causing so much damage, loss and confusion as to make it manifest abroad that the British in Cyprus are no longer in control of the situation.

The above objective will be attained:

1. By sabotage of Government installations and military camps.
2. By surprise attacks of small and highly mobile combat units against the British forces.
3. By organizing the passive resistance of the population.

Because of the difficulty of conducting a systematic, large-scale armed guerrilla campaign, and in view of the fact that the territory is not capable of absorbing large guerrilla forces, the main weight of the campaign will be placed on sabotage.

The military task of the combat units will have as its principal aim the cover and support of the saboteurs' work, as well as to confuse and divert the attention of the British administration in Cyprus.

Should events take a favourable turn, and always provided that sufficient weapons are available, one should not exclude the possibility of the armed struggle increasing in both scale and intensity.

Action under the three forms mentioned above, if it is to attain its object, cannot be confined to minor and intermittent operations against insignificant targets but must involve a vigorous and continuous campaign aimed at getting important results.

It should not be supposed that by these means we should expect to impose a total defeat on the British forces in Cyprus. Our purpose is to win a moral victory through a process of attrition, by harassing, confusing and finally exasperating the enemy forces, with the object of achieving our main aim as defined in the first paragraph of this plan.

In addition to these activities, we shall take measures to neutralize all opposition in Cyprus, from whatever quarter, as well as to put out of action and severely punish any Cypriots acting as British agents to the prejudice of our struggle.

The support of the whole Greek nation is essential to our cause. It may have a decisive effect on our fortunes. Such moral support should demonstrate the solidarity of all free Greeks with their enslaved brethren.

This support in Greece should:

1. Follow up our revolutionary action in Cyprus with organized demonstrations in all Greek cities: first, to applaud our successes; second, to denounce to the civilized world the acts of violence and oppression committed by the British in Cyprus against the civil population; finally, to demonstrate in the most solemn manner the Greek people's determination to help the Cypriot struggle by all the means in their power.

2. Enlighten public opinion through the world by such means as leaflets and Press propaganda.

The preparation and execution of the above programme shall be carried out by a specially constituted Athens Committee.

SABOTAGE

Sabotage will be undertaken by special groups which will preferably remain in the town and village areas where they will operate. Only in the imminent danger of discovery shall the groups or some of their members withdraw to places fixed in advance for each group; and from there, if need be, to the mountain areas where the guerrilla units are stationed.

Targets will be selected by the Leader himself in view of their importance and that of the expected results. Co-operation, where necessary, between sabotage groups and combat units will also be decided by the Leader. Each unit will be under the immediate orders of its own commander who will take his orders from the Leader.

Saboteurs will carry pistols and hand grenades. They will use time-bombs, dynamite, anti-personnel and ordinary mines; also, possibly, magnetic mines.

The formation of the sabotage groups, their stations, the storing of their supplies, etc., will be carefully studied and fixed by the Leader himself who will make a preliminary reconnaissance of Cyprus before the movement starts.

Initially, there will be one sabotage group for each of the following districts: Nicosia, Famagusta, Dhekelia, Larnaca, Limasol, Episkopi, Paphos, Kyrenia, Lapithos and Pedhoulas-Lefka.

GUERRILLA SHOCK GROUPS

The mission of these groups will be:

1. To assist the saboteurs either with cover and support, on a pre-determined plan, or by harassing the British forces and cutting their lines of communication so as to facilitate the saboteurs' work.

2. To harass the police posts and neutralize their action.

3. Eventually to carry out more important missions against military targets, should circumstances permit.

The guerrilla shock groups may be called upon to increase their activities. It would therefore be advisable to build up a plentiful store of arms in the island.

FORMATION OF SHOCK GROUPS. Initially 5 shock groups will be formed: 3 in the Olympus area, 1 in the Pentadactylos range and 1 in reserve. The groups will be as follows:

1. *Olympus Groups.* Commander ....[1]

(*a*) Kykko-Stavros area. Sector: the road between Lefka, Pedhoulas, Kykko monastery and Stavros. Force: 8 men. Armament: 1 bren, 2 stens, 8 rifles.

(*b*) Khrysoroyiatissa monastery area. Sector: from the town of Khrysokhou to Kykko monastery, Prodromos, Platres and Kourion. Force: 10 men. Armament: 1 bren, 1 tommy gun, 2 stens, 6 rifles.

(*c*) Troodos area. Sector: Kakopetria, Ayios Epiphanios, Makheras monastery, Lefkara. The boundary on the west to be that of the Khrysoroyiatissa group. Force and armaments as Khrysoroyiatissa group.

2. *Pentadactylos Group.* Sector: Kyrenian mountain range from Apostolos Andreas to Myrtou and Lapithos. Force: 10 men. Armament: 2 brens, 1 tommy gun, 4 stens, 10 rifles. This group will be divided into 3 sub-groups.

[1] *Translator's note.* All the commanders' names have been left blank in the original text.

Note: The formation of the shock groups has been determined on the basis of the quantity of weapons available to us today. Minor adjustments might be made in the event of more arms becoming available later.

3. *Reserve Group.* Armament: the heavy machine guns, 1 tommy gun, 8 stens, 22 rifles.

This will either reinforce the shock groups or sabotage groups or else will form fresh shock groups in areas which may need them as the struggle develops. The positioning of the reserve will be determined as circumstances demand.

Each shock group should have its own permanent centre, which should however be changed from time to time within the sector, in order to make discovery and pursuit by the enemy more difficult. Each group within the sector should also organize its own hide-out to serve either as a base of operations or as a more easily defended place of refuge that permits of escape in the event of an attack by superior forces. The above considerations should govern the choice of hide-out.

The tactics to be followed by the group if attacked by superior forces will not be to stand and fight back (unless there are orders to the contrary) but to mislead and confuse the enemy, and then escape. The group may even break up so as to enable the men to escape singly or in pairs and go into hiding. A regrouping point should be chosen in advance where the group can re-form when the danger is past.

All the above shock groups will be supplied with mines to enable them to blow up roads etc.

Note: I do not believe the number of shock groups should be more than above, at any rate initially. For a higher number would make it harder for them to hide or to get away in the event of an attack. The terrain should appear empty so as to make discovery difficult by British search forces; passing through the enemy lines and escape will also thus be facilitated. We should aim at increasing our numbers only if the course of the struggle requires it and provided we can secure all the conditions necessary for successful operations, including facilities for concealment and escape.

ORGANIZATION OF PASSIVE RESISTANCE

To attain our objectives, simultaneously with our combat activities we shall organize passive resistance among the population so that we can anywhere and at any time upset and neutralize the working of the British administration in all fields, and correspondingly raise the national morale and the Cypriots' power of resistance.

This means organizing the population into a single internal front to boycott the British and their Cypriot agents (the latter must also be shadowed and special groups will undertake the execution of any person considered dangerous to the cause); to organize protest demonstrations against oppressive Government measures; and to enlighten public opinion abroad about the happenings in Cyprus. For the last purpose an Information Service will supply information to the Athens Committee which will see that due publicity is given; the illegal Press will keep the Cypriot people informed.

Organization of civilians will be by districts, with a responsible leader in each.

INTELLIGENCE CENTRES

Special centres will amass intelligence on British troop movements in Cyprus; on military targets to be neutralized; on movements and activities of the enemy so that we can counteract all activity directed against the struggle. The Leader will pass on all intelligence reaching him to certain fixed transmission centres. The plan provides for the initial functioning of one such centre in each district.

SUPPLIES

Each group will obtain its food supplies through local agents who will deposit the supplies at spots fixed in advance which must be at some distance from the group's base. In addition, each group should have within its area a reserve stock of tinned food for emergency; any consumed should be made good as soon as possible.

GENERAL

Suitable hide-outs must be found in houses or other premises in towns and villages for persons who have a mission in the vicinity or are wanted by the authorities and are in danger of arrest. To select these will be the duty of all units as well as of all in charge of branches of the Command.

PRELIMINARY PREPARATIONS

1. Dispatch of the arms, now ready, to Cyprus.
2. Immediate departure of the Leader for Cyprus where he will see to the detailed organization and preparation of all of the objectives laid down in the Plan, and will draw up instructions in detail for the various groups and formations. This requires at least three months.
3. Arrangements for supplying the revolutionary committee in Cyprus with everything required for the struggle so that this shall not suffer through lack of material support.
4. The establishing of a Benevolent Fund to provide for the families of victims of the struggle.

II

Plan T–P[1]

Turkish activity in the towns may take the form either of demonstrations by a Turkish mob leading to the firing or other destruction of Greek shops, accompanied by the murder of Greeks; or of attacks, especially at night, on Greek property, carried out by Turkish auxiliary police or by Turkish youths with police connivance.

DEFENSIVE MEASURES TO BE TAKEN

1. In the event of mob demonstrations, the occupation of vantage-points on the route to be followed by the Turkish mob which our men will attack with bombs. In choosing and occupying these posts the following points should be taken into account:

(*a*) The posts taken should be in the upper storeys of houses or on house-tops; not in the street itself or at street level. By being high up one has better opportunities for attack as well as greater safety; down in the street these chances are much smaller.

(*b*) Positions taken up should preferably be at the beginning of the mob's route to prevent them penetrating into a Greek quarter; also at a narrow point where it will be difficult for the Turkish hooligans to get away; thus the confusion will be greater.

(*c*) The members of our groups should be stationed in depth at five or six points along the route.

Finally there should be no Greeks about in the street. The emptier the streets are the easier it will be to throw bombs.

Each sector should prepare a plan for submission to myself comprising the following: probable routes to be followed by a Turkish mob; points to be occupied by our men for the attack; any suggestions the particular sector may offer. The memorandum should be accompanied by a street plan.

2. Night attacks by Turkish auxiliary police cannot be dealt with so effectively: there will be a curfew and the auxiliary police will be in small groups able to move about without arousing suspicion.

The shopkeeper's best protection will be to organize a special body to guard their shops. They should ask the authorities' permission and should hold them responsible, if they refuse, for any damage caused. The result of such a move should be reported to me as soon as possible.

[1] T-P: the Greek initials of 'Turks' and 'Towns'.

Appendix

The plans for each sector's defence shall be put into action only after approval by me.

(signed) DIGHENIS

Note: The execution of this plan was entrusted to the special anti-Turkish groups.

III

General Instructions for the Self-Defence of the Greek Population against Turkish Attacks

The following are my general instructions for the Greek inhabitants' defence against Turkish attacks in the towns.

Places of assembly, special duties and leaders must be fixed beforehand to avoid misunderstandings and for the more effective use of the Greek population in self-defence. The assembly points should be behind each town's line of defence as fixed in Plan T–P. A single leader should be appointed to command each of the groups, which will assemble at the selected points. He will give directions and guidance. No one shall have the right to move or take any action without the leader's orders. The group leaders will receive instructions from the responsible person appointed by yourselves for the armed defence of the town.

I think it advisable that you should get into touch with the new guilds and other organizations or associations which will be able to designate suitable persons to act as leaders and to assist you in the organization of the inhabitants' rapid assembly.

Once assembled, the population should intervene in the following circumstances. If our armed defence groups are already in position, the inhabitants will either reinforce certain points, where necessary, or, in the event of a Turkish mob having already succeeded in passing our men's stations, they must hold them back. In the event of the Turks being defeated and forced to retreat, our people will pursue them and take reprisals.

Our people must be in a position to cope with any other emergency that may arise from other Turkish activity, such as the secret entry into a town of Turks or auxiliary police.

If our armed defence groups have not time to take up their positions because the enemy has got ahead of them, the population must try to advance to meet the mob wherever possible and defend themselves until our armed groups have had time to intervene.

97

The following points are essential to this: systematic co-operation and consultation with the various organizations and unions; selection of suitable persons to act as leaders at the assembly points; absolute obedience of the inhabitants to the orders of the leaders in order to avoid confusion and possible panic.

These are the general lines of my ideas. I desire you to put them into execution and report to me, at the same time submitting a plan of the places where the population will assemble.

(signed) DIGHENIS

IV

Instructions for Village Defence against Turkish Attacks

It is difficult to anticipate the exact direction of danger, for the enemy may approach from one direction or he may by-pass the village and attack from any other direction he may choose as being more convenient. Consequently each village must be organized to be able to face attack from any direction. Obviously, however, there will be one or more directions which will be more dangerous and others less so. So we must be prepared to oppose the enemy most effectively at the more dangerous points, by being stronger there both in defensive preparation and in numbers. It is not difficult to determine which these points are.

To be able to meet every contingency, we may take into account the following and make the necessary dispositions: firstly, it is essential to keep a constant advanced look-out to inform us of the approach, strength and direction of the enemy; secondly, defensive dispositions should be studied on the basis of the following factors:

1. *If the village has an all-Greek population and we have sufficient forces:* we will occupy and defend the approaches to the village according to the priorities laid down in the first paragraph of these instructions. A large part of our forces should be kept in reserve in the centre of the village to reinforce any threatened point. Should our defence prove strong enough, part or the whole of this reserve force should issue from the village and counter-attack taking the opponent in the rear and driving him out.

2. *If the village is all-Greek but the forces at our disposal are limited:* we should occupy certain points only, fixed in advance and defending the most dangerous approaches. The remainder of our forces, kept in reserve, should be ready to hasten to points threatened as the enemy attack develops. Possibly a part of our reserve forces, if conditions are favourable and the enemy is not in strength, may counter-attack as in 1 above.

Appendix

3. *In a village with a mixed Greek and Turkish population:* it is essential first of all to safeguard one's defence against the internal enemy, either by completely neutralizing his activity as soon as the approach of the external enemy is announced; or, should this not be possible either through lack of time or because the internal enemy is too strong, by occupying from the start certain positions within the village and maintaining a constant defensive to prevent all attempts by the internal foe to move in the direction of the Greek quarter. The rest of our forces should be disposed so as to occupy certain points at the approaches to the Greek quarter; some should be kept in reserve. After taking the above measures against the internal enemy, the defence will follow the pattern of 1 or 2 above, depending on whether we still dispose of sufficient forces.

It is therefore essential that each village has a plan of defence. Some may think this unnecessary in the case of villages which are not near enemy villages. This view is mistaken. For, on the one hand, we can never know exactly what may happen, and, on the other, attacks against villages may well be carried out by auxiliary police at the instigation of the British.

As I have emphasized in a previous order, we should use fire-arms, if at all, only on a very limited scale. For the enemy may try to provoke us into bringing out our arms. Hand grenades, which are highly effective, should be used instead.

Fire-arms are to be used only in taking reprisals for an attack on a village, in which case our special groups will carry the necessary arms, for they will be able to withdraw immediately and hide them.

I wish to suggest the following supplementary measures as necessary for village defence:

Members of our Organization who find themselves in a village from which hostile forces are setting out or who anywhere notice their presence, must alert the threatened village in good time.

Should the enemy be using vehicles, arrangements must be made to mine the roads he will use.

Usually any small group, armed with rifles, which succeeds in concealing itself and firing at the enemy from the rear, just at the moment when the latter is attacking a village, will succeed in causing panic.

(signed) DIGHENIS

V

Instructions for Ambushes

Ambushes and sabotage constitute our two main methods of combat. They require careful study, and each instance will have its appropriate methods. These are my instructions for ambushes:

Guerrilla Warfare

1. We should make the widest possible use of mines and 'small cannon' Both are very effective, one avoids wasting the ammunition of automatic weapons and one need only employ a very small number of men. Escape is easy and casualties are kept to a minimum. Percussion mines should be used on non-asphalted roads where there is little traffic, or at times when there are few private cars. Percussion mines are most effective and do not call for the presence of men to set them off. 'Small cannon' also are very effective, provided a suitable position is chosen where they can be set up and fired at the right moment. The successful use of both weapons depends on proper training. It is therefore my wish that all our men undergo intensive training in the use of these weapons which in my opinion both achieve results and are economical from the point of view of numbers.

2. There is a general tendency to employ large quantities of material and men in ambushes. This is a great mistake. The results obtained by an ambush depend on the element of surprise combined with making good use of limited means at suitable sites. The combined use of a 'small cannon' and automatic weapons is essential both to increase the ambush's chances of success and to reduce the number of men and weapons used to a minimum. Shotguns are very effective in ambushes, although I notice a tendency to prefer automatic weapons. That is a mistake and results in a wasteful consumption of ammunition.

3. The duration of an ambush attack cannot and should not exceed about five minutes. For should the enemy not be completely neutralized, we run the risk of finding ourselves caught inside his converging fire and so being unable to escape. When attacking an enemy motor vehicle, we should keep a watch on its companions and engage their attention, as the chances are that the soldiers inside will alight and seek to cut off our retreat. Generally speaking, the question of our retreat after the engagement should be studied from the moment we set the ambush. A path of escape must be constantly borne in mind.

4. Mixed ambushes employing automatic weapons, a 'small cannon' and mines should mostly take place at night, for then there are better opportunities of surprise and escape. In daytime ambushes are best set in precipitous and thickly-wooded areas, where there are good chances of being able to get away and observation from helicopters is more difficult. In daytime too it is advisable to use percussion mines and 'small cannon'. Percussion mines were employed in certain sectors with excellent results and their use should be generalized as far as possible.

5. The above instructions should be studied by the sectors and their men trained to apply them in the appropriate circumstances.

(signed) DIGHENIS

Appendix

VI

Explosives made in Cyprus

EXPLOSIVE AND INCENDIARY MIXTURES MANUFACTURED FROM MATERIALS AVAILABLE IN CYPRUS

1. EXPLOSIVE

   (a) 100 parts potassium chlorate, 20 parts urotropine.
   Detonated by ordinary or electric detonator.
   (b) 96 parts potassium chlorate, 12 parts manganous peroxide (pyrolusite).
   Detonated by ordinary or electric detonator.
   (c) 88 parts potassium chlorate, 12 parts vaseline.
   Detonated by ordinary or electric detonator. A wick can also be used.
   (d) 78 parts potassium chlorate, 12 parts potassium nitrate, 6 parts sulphur, 4 parts carbon, 20 parts urotropine.
   A first-class mixture. Detonated by ordinary or electric detonator.

2. INCENDIARY

   75 parts potassium chlorate, 25 parts sugar.
   The results are both incendiary and explosive. The explosive or incendiary power depends on the proportions in the mixture. If one desires a bigger explosive capacity, use a higher proportion of potassium chlorate; if incendiary, use a higher proportion of sugar.

PREPARATION OF FULMINATE OF MERCURY

We had to use a simple and safe method, because we lacked scientifically perfect apparatus, equipment for temperature control and regulation of flow tables, etc. Furthermore we had to produce on an industrial basis.

1. *Nitrosis.* Use bottles of chemically pure nitric acid with a specific gravity of 1·42. These bottles should have a capacity of 1 kg. Remove the stoppers and place 120 gr. of chemically pure mercury in each bottle. The mixture is left for 12 hours overnight for the mercury to dissolve completely. Then the bottles are stoppered and gently turned upside down for complete mixing. Now and then remove the stoppers for a while in order to reduce the pressure of any vapours, and then replace the stoppers.

2. Pour alcohol of 95° into large wide-mouthed receptacles (preferably demijohns) in the proportion of 1 oke (1·28 kg. or 2·823 lb.) for each bottle in process 1 above, and transfer the product of process 1 to the demijohns. (Demijohns are without stoppers.) In a very short time a strong reaction starts accompanied by the emission of strongly pungent fumes.

When the fumes cease the reaction is complete and the fulminate of mercury is precipitated at the bottom of the demijohns. Wash the product in distilled water and dry on glass.

MANUFACTURE OF DETONATORS

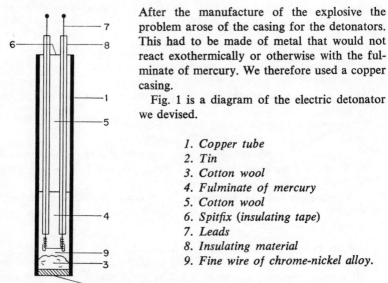

After the manufacture of the explosive the problem arose of the casing for the detonators. This had to be made of metal that would not react exothermically or otherwise with the fulminate of mercury. We therefore used a copper casing.

Fig. 1 is a diagram of the electric detonator we devised.

1. *Copper tube*
2. *Tin*
3. *Cotton wool*
4. *Fulminate of mercury*
5. *Cotton wool*
6. *Spitfix (insulating tape)*
7. *Leads*
8. *Insulating material*
9. *Fine wire of chrome-nickel alloy.*

Fig. 1

MANUFACTURE OF BOMBS

Afxentiou cocktail bomb (BKA), explosive and incendiary.

1. *Small flask filled with a mixture of*
   potassium chlorate and sugar
2. *Test tube filled with sulphuric acid*
3. *Cast iron rod*
4. *Lead weight*
5. *Spitfix or sticking plaster*
6. *Cork soaked in paraffin.*

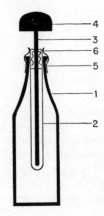

Fig. 2

102

Appendix

When the test tube (2) breaks, the sulphuric acid it contains comes into contact with the incendiary mixture in the flask (1), automatically producing an explosion and flames. To achieve this, a piece of lead (4) is fixed to the portion of the rod (3) protruding from the cork. Firstly, the lead through its weight makes the BKA fall head on; secondly, as it strikes the ground it jerks the iron rod to which it is attached, which breaks the test tube full of sulphuric acid, thereby causing the automatic explosion and ignition of the mixture.

This bomb was used in different forms and variations, like those shown in Figs. 3 and 4 below.

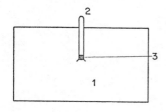

Fig. 3

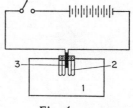

Fig. 4

INCENDIARY TIME BOMB

1. *Container with mixture of potassium chlorate and sugar*
2. *Test tube with sulphuric acid*
3. *Cork stopper*

ELECTRICALLY DETONATED INCENDIARY BOMB

1. *Container with potassium chlorate and sugar*
2. *Test tubes with sulphuric acid stoppered with paraffin-soaked corks*
3. *Electric detonator*

In Fig. 3 the time of ignition depends on the thickness of the stopper (3); for with the passage of time the sulphuric acid corrodes the stopper and comes into contact with the explosive and incendiary mixture.

VII

Percussion Mines

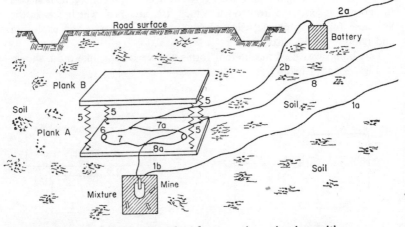

Fig. 5. Section of road with percussion mine in position

The percussion mine consists of the following parts: the mine itself with the explosive mixture and the electric detonator; two planks A and B; a battery, wires, etc.

METHOD OF MANUFACTURE

1. The mine itself. Place the explosive mixture into a container with strong sides – of tubing or thick sheet iron. Reinforce the mixture with a small amount of fulminate of mercury or even dynamite. One may even include a few ordinary detonators to increase the explosive power. The quantity of the mixture required if the mine is to be used against vehicles is 5-6 okes (6·4-7·68 kg. or 14·115-16·938 lb.).

Then put the electric detonator with the two wires 1a and 1b inside the container with the explosive mixture inside. Attach it firmly so that it does not protrude and get displaced. The mine is now ready.

2. Planks A and B. Take a plank (A), the dimensions of which should be such that when it is laid on a road at least one of the wheels of a vehicle is bound to pass over it. At the four corners of plank A attach four springs (5). The strength of these springs must be determined so that their compression bringing about the contact of the upper plank (B) with the switches on plank A corresponds to the weight of the target we wish to attack. If, for example, we want to attack vehicles only, not individuals, the springs must be able to bear a weight of 80-100 okes (102·4-128 kg. or 225·84-282·3 lb.) before contact is made.

In the middle of the two ends of plank A fix two switches (6) connected by two wires (7, 7a). We use *two* switches, instead of one at the middle of the plank, to make sure the mine is detonated even if the target puts pressure on only one of them.

Above plank A place a second plank (B), of the same dimensions, so as to be in contact with the four springs. Wrap both planks in nylon to prevent earth, stones, etc., being wedged in between them when they are being camouflaged. Otherwise plank B will be prevented from compressing the springs, and consequently the switches of plank A, when the target goes over the mine.

3. Battery. One may use a battery capable of giving a current of 6 volts (for example, 2 flat torch batteries). However, it depends mainly on the resistance of the detonator. It is therefore essential to check the voltage required by the detonator used.

Before placing the mine underground, connect the wires as follows: connect wire 7 with 1b (one of the two wires leading to the electric detonator inside the mine). Connect wire 7a with wire 2b which is brought into contact with one of the poles of the battery. To close the circuit the other wire of the detonator (1a) is extended as far as required and left free. The other pole of the battery is connected with wire 2a, which is also extended as far as required and left free. Finally at point 8a, where wire 7 is connected with wire 1b, connect wire 8 and extend it in the direction of wire 2a.

Laying of the Mine and Planks

The mine itself is laid in an excavation made in the road, of sufficient depth and breadth to hold the mine and the two planks. The two planks are laid in the excavation as explained in section 2 of 'Method of Manufacture'. The mine can be placed either below the planks or at one side of them, but in any case near the centre of the road so that when the mine is detonated the explosion takes place directly underneath the vehicle.

When the mine and planks are in position the surface must be carefully camouflaged to remove all suspicious traces of digging. This is something most important, for mines are usually discovered from such traces.

Control and Working

The mine can be detonated either automatically (and so with no person present), or with someone there to detonate the mine at the moment of the vehicle passing over it.

Control is carried out as follows: connect wires 2a and 8. If a spark is produced (one can also use a small torch bulb and see if it lights), it means that the planks have already pressed the two switches and that therefore the mine will explode as soon as we connect wires 1a and 2a. If the mine is being detonated by personal control, the operator must connect wires 1a and 2a as soon as the target is passing over the mine. If the mine is to be detonated automatically, the planks must be arranged so as not to be pressing the switches. This can be ascertained if no spark is produced after the connection of wires 2a and 8. In that case connect wires 1a and 2a and move away. The passage of the target over the mine will automatically produce the explosion.

The three wires 1a, 2a and 8 must not be confused. To avoid this it is advisable to wrap a coil of wire round 1a and at the same time be careful not to bring it into contact with 2a. Wire 8 should have a knot on it to distinguish it when we connect it with 2a to make sure whether or not the switches are pressed when the planks are in position.

VIII

Extract from a British Note on the conclusions drawn from Operation 'Mare's Nest' (28 January 1959)

Air-planning. For this operation we planned to fly in by helicopter some 16 OPs [Observation Points]. The advantage of flying OPs is that it gives one a quick control of the area whilst the deployment of the remainder of the troops, which is unavoidably slow, takes place. We used both RAF Sycamores and JHU Whirlwinds for this. There is nothing difficult in planning a large-scale fly-in of this sort, but the point to remember is that it must be done in the most meticulous detail. It needs a separate conference which should be attended by the officer (of Brigade Headquarters) who will be running the helicopter strip, the officer in charge of each battalion's fly-in parties and the helicopter Flight Commanders. Attached is a *pro forma*[1] which this Brigade and 284 Helicopter Squadron RAF have worked out and used for some 18 months for operations of this type.

I have always found it necessary to use the following 'Path-finder' technique for this type of operation. The technique is simple and is as follows:

Each battalion produces one 'Path-finding' officer who leads the battalion allotment of helicopters, and on the first sortie he puts down one man to each OP. The one man has with him a fluorescent panel which he displays immediately on landing. The build-up is then done by individual helicopters on to these single men. This puts the responsibility for the map-

[1] See page 108.

reading firmly on to the battalion doing it, which must be right; the helicopter pilot has to fly the machine and cannot be in the full military picture.

Cases often arise in which the OP, which has been pre-selected from map and air photo, is not in fact suitable for a man to be put down by helicopter and some small adjustment of position has to be made. This adjustment clearly must be made by an Army officer, which can be done using this 'Path-finder' technique.

It must always be remembered that the use of the air is a bonus to one's planning and that weather conditions may preclude flying. One must always have an alternative plan.

Deployment. It must be remembered in an operation of this sort that deployment will of necessity be very slow. It will in fact go at the speed of a marching soldier with a 60 lb. load on his back, climbing a very steep hill. You must plan for it to go slowly, and I am sure that if you try to go too quickly you may well get into an administrative muddle which may take three days to sort out.

In fact on this operation the weather was excessively unkind to us, and it took us two full days really to achieve our planned deployment. As a matter of interest we were only able to fly in two OP parties, as the excessive atmospheric turbulence prevented helicopter pilots from holding a hover, and this made it unsafe for loaded soldiers to go down the rope out of helicopters. . . .

Air. We had a great deal of air effort in support. During the operation we used Sycamores and Whirlwind helicopters, and Auster, Chipmunk and Pioneer aircraft. The first lesson that I learnt was the need for efficient ground control of all these aircraft and for controlled planning of their activities. We started with a tentacle, and with the Duty Officer in the Operations Room trying to run the air net and air requests in addition to his other duties. It was quickly apparent that this was impossible, and that we were not making economical use of the aircraft. We therefore borrowed the GLO [Ground Liaison Officer] and set up a proper Air Office from which the GLO controlled the aircraft and planned the next day's sorties and requests. This developed quickly and easily into an efficient process, and we found that we could reduce the number of sorties required.

284 Squadron (*Sycamores*), who are very experienced at Cyprus internal security operations, gave us the most excellent service and were as good as ever. I think ground troops have still got something to learn in the choosing and preparation of helicopter LZs [Landing Zones] in bad country.

Whirlwinds. These were flown by pilots of the JHU who, although experienced, are mostly new to Cyprus. They learnt the technique very quickly, and gave us extremely good service.

Austers. We had permanent Auster patrols flying over the whole area. These patrols produced a great deal of valuable information, and found quite a number of caves, and of movement in forests within the area. With their excellent wireless communications they were able to direct ground patrols on to anything suspicious they found. It was interesting that it took the pilots two days' hard flying really to get to know the area. The Auster, of course, has a 62 set which works direct on a brigade or battalion command net, a crystal set which works to the tentacle, and we also got good results from both 88 and 31 sets working direct to patrols and OPs on the ground.

Chipmunks. These were used, like the Austers, for patrolling. Observation from them was excellent. At the moment they suffer from the limitation of only having a crystal-controlled wireless which means they can report back to the tentacle but not direct to troops on the ground.

Pioneers. We achieved successful results from dropping supplies from these aircraft. We were starting from scratch, as neither pilots nor dispatchers had any previous practice at this. Standard of accuracy improved rapidly. At the end we were having complete recovery of supplies dropped on to knife-edged ridges with very little damage to the containers. We have not yet got the right containers for dropping fluids, and all experiments with jerrycans were unsuccessful. The party receiving supplies on a knife-edged ridge is well advised to make a small Dannert fence each side of the crest line to stop Compo etc. rolling down to the bottom of the hill.

Pro forma (see p. 106)

To 3 Indep. Inf. Bde. Standing Orders for IS dated 16 November 1957

Unit....   GR of LZ   Time of arrival of Hel. at LZ....
Operation....   LZ marking   Time of take-off first sortie....
Date....   Tps to arrive at LZ by....

Hel. No.	Sortie No.	Destination		Load		Remarks
		Posn	Grid ref.	Passengers	Kit and stores	

Appendix

IX

List of Abbreviations Used in Text

ANE	EOKA Young Stalwarts
EAEM	United Unbroken National Front
EOKA	National Organization of Cyprus Fighters
EOX	Special Hand-Grenade Groups
OA	Defence Groups
OKT	Shotgun Commando Groups
PEKA	Political Committee of the Cypriot Struggle